AF553715

Adolescence Education

Adolescence Education

Editor
Dr. Digumarti Bhaskara Rao

M.Sc., M.A., M.A., M.Ed., Ph. D.
R.V.R. College of Education
Guntur -522006,
Andhra Pradesh, India.

Discovery Publishing House
New Delhi, 110002 (India)

Published by:

DISCOVERY PUBLISHING HOUSE PVT. LTD.
4383/4B, Ansari Road, Darya Ganj
New Delhi-110 002 (India)
Phone : +91-11-23279245; 23253475; 43596065
E-mail : discoverybooksindia@gmail.com
discoverypublishinghouse@gmail.com
namitwasan9@gmail.com
web : www.discoverypublishinggroup.com

***First Published:* 1998**
***Reprinted:* 2022**

ISBN: 978-81-7141-432-1

Adolescence Education

Printed at:
Infinity Imaging Systems
Delhi

PREFACE

One of the dramatic changes of life is the transition from childhood into adolescence. In a very short time, the child takes on an adult-like physique and intellect. Adolescence, according to some, is a peaceful period to make decisions about who one is and how one is to live one's life and, according to some other, is a time of great stress as one has to keep one's psychological balance as he/she is considered neither a child nor an adult. Whatever the physical and or psychological strains and stresses may be the adolescent has to make his/her presence in the society in a decent way as he/she is a social animal. To be a good social being, adolescent needs adequate information about adolescence.

To guide the adolescents, adolescence education is necessary. This book is intended to educate the adolescents in the aspects concerned to happy adolescent living. This book—with a package of four modules on Physical Aspects, Social Aspects, Sex Roles and Sexually Transmitted Diseases—will give adequate knowledge and right direction to adolescents in leading their adolescent life peacefully and meaningfully.

Dr. Digumarti Bhaskara Rao
R. V. R. College of Education
Nagarjuna University
Guntur

ACKNOWLEDGEMENTS

I am grateful to the UNESCO Principal Regional Office for Asia and the Pacific, Bangkok for giving me the necessary permission to use the package on Adolescence Education.

I am thankful to Prof. D. E. Torrijos for the prompt and courteous replies wheneven I contacted either for material or for information.

I am also thankful to all the personalities who worked for the development of this package on adolescence education and the UNESCO personnel for their efforts in adding flesh and blood to different dimensions of adolescence education.

Dr. Digumarti Bhaskara Rao
Secretary, ACCESS.

CONTENTS

INTRODUCTION

The family is one of the basic institutions of mankind and thus serves as the focal point of national programmes on populations education in the region. A few countries like Malaysia, Indonesia, the Philippines, Thailand and Vietnam, have refocused their programme thrust so that family life education objectives and concepts will have a broader coverage. In these countries, family life education as part of population education is aimed at: (1) a better understanding of the physical and emotional changes associated with growing up; (2) establishing and maintaining personal relationships among the family, friends and society at large; and (3) developing knowledge and values related to successful marriage, childbearing and rearing, and other aspects of family development.

One of the major parts of family life education deals with adolescent fertility, which is an emerging concern in the developing countries . Data from the population Reference Bureau estimate that 60 per cent of the population in developing countries is under 25 years of age and 40 per cent is under 15. At least, 13 million births occur to adolescents every year. Worldwide, there were about 245 million women aged 15-19 in 1985. 82 per cent lived in the developing countries and three-quarters of these in Asia. This figure is projected to increase by 75 million in the developing countries by the year 2020.

While some countries still have a low average age at marriage, this age is increasing in many countries. On the other hand, as a result of improved nutrition and health, young people nowadays are reaching physical maturity earlier and girls experience their menarche at a much younger age. While the increasing age at marriage is fulfilling the attainment of delayed marriage, which is one of the objectives of population education, late marriage is giving rise to some problems related to adolescent fertility in some countries. These problems in some countries include teenage pregnancies, illegal abortions and illegitimate births. Teen-age pregnancies and births are in turn associated with increased health risks to the mother and infant, curtailed education, reduced employment potential, and high population growth rate.

These problems have generated a very high interest in developing programmes on family life education, and have triggered off increasing demands for information and materials in this field. Regardless of the controversy that may surround them, programmes on adolescent counseling and family life education are being seriously considered by an increasing number of countries. The result is the development of relevant packages on adolescence education

This package on Adolescence Education is meant to serve as a practical resource guide, primarily for teachers and secondarily for trainers, guidance counsellors and youth workers, who are engaged in teaching, training and communicating family life education concepts to adolescents. More specifically, this package is aimed at strengthening their professional skills in: (i) assisting young people acquire the knowledge, skills and values which will prepare them for the responsibilities of adult life, marriage, parenthood and participation in the life of the community, and thus contributing to healthy and satisfying lives; (ii) Contributing to the development of the individual so as to promote happiness and responsible behaviour; (iii) helping young people to understand their feeling and beliefs and to cope with the physical, emotional and social changes which are part of growing up, enabling them to recognize what is important and to behave in a way which is caring and responsible; and (iv) helping young people learn how to communicate effectively with other and to make wise decisions about all matters connected with family life, personal relationships, and membership in the community.

This package consists of the following modules:

Module One: Physical Aspects

deals with the male and female reproductive systems; the physical, emotional and psychological changes that occur during puberty and the physiological processes of human conception.

Module Two: Social Aspects

covers topics on sexual behaviour, sexuality in childhood and adolescence, love, dating and relationship, adolescent pregnancy and moral code of ethics.

Module Three: Sex Roles

deals with role expectations, male and female roles and sex stereotyping.

Module Four. Sexually Transmitted Diseases

discusses the various types of STD, their origins, symptoms, effects, testing and prevention and explains them in the contexts of social and medical problems.

Each module comprises several lessons. Each lessons is provided with a set of objectives and indicates the time required for teaching, the materials to be used and the set of procedures. Information sheets to help teachers in expanding the subject, and activities/exercises for students are also provided.

Conceptual Framework for Adolescence Education Programme

Adolescence education is an educational programme designed to provide learners with adequate and accurate knowledge about human sexuality in its biological, psychological, socio-cultural and moral dimensions. Adolescence education focuses largely, though not exclusively, on the individual-on self-awareness, personal relationships, human sexual development, reproduction and sexual behaviour.[1] Human sexuality as the core of adolescence education is a function of the total personality, which includes the human reproductive system and processes, attitudes towards being a women or a man, and relationships among members of the same sex and the opposite sex.[2] It embraces the biological, psychological, socio-cultural and ethical aspects of human sexual behaviour. It helps people to understand their sexuality, to learn to respect others as sexual beings, and to make responsible decisions about their behaviour. Following is a brief description of the main components of adolescence education.

1. Physical Aspects

In most countries, among the crucial topics taken up in the Biology course are the anatomy and physiology of the human reproductive system. Anatomy refers to the science of the structure of the human body, and the interrelations of their parts. In adolescence education, the anatomy of the human reproductive system - male vis-a-vis the female—is an interesting filed of study. Physiology of the reproductive system refers to a study of the processes and mechanisms by which parts of the reproductive system function. it is extremely important for boys and girls to know about their bodies and how these function. Misinformation, or lack of information, often results in unnecessary worries and may cause serious problems. For instance, many young girls without proper education about menstruation are shocked to find themselves bleeding at one stage during puberty. On the other hand, untutored young boys may be upset by their wet dreams.

Wet dreams are an indication of the ability of a young man to cause conception, while the onset of menstruation indicates that a young woman is capable of conceiving a child.

Under physical aspect, the following sub-topics are included:

a) Anatomy and physiology of the reproductive systems

This part identifies the various parts of the male and female reproductive anatomy and their functions. Adolescents need this information in order to understand successive lesson concerning conception, pregnancy and contraception. A lesson on the menstrual cycle is included.

b) Physical, emotional and psychological changes during puberty

Puberty is a time for physical and emotional change.[3] During puberty, adolescents begin to get concerned about the physical changes they see in their bodies. Some may be developing at a slower or a faster rate than their friends. Some may be feeling awkward about their growth. Some may be anxious over their bodily changes and may have conflicting feeling about becoming adults. Others may feel proud and comfortable about their approach to maturity.

It is also at this time that adolescents develop their self-esteem. Adolescence is a period of high stress for many people. Students are much concerned about their physical image and their relationships with their family and friends. Their confusion, concern and anxiety affect their feeling of self-worth. Behaviour matches self-image. A young person with a positive, healthy self-image will make positive, healthy choices.[4] This unit contains lessons which encourage self-awareness and self acceptance.

c) Conception, pregnancy and birth

This topic is aimed at familiarizing the students with basic knowledge concerning the physiological processes involved in conception, pregnancy and birth. it is very important that adolescents should know this topic because, much as the authorities would like to ignore the problem, in many countries adolescent pregnancy is on the increase.[5]

In many countries in Asia early marriage is common. Young couples are urged to have a child as soon as possible or to achieve pregnancy within a year after marrying to confirm the husband's manhood and the wife's capability to produce a child. Early pregnancies create a lot of health, social and psychological risks. The younger the mother, the more serious the physical consequences of pregnancy are likely to be. Complications in pregnancy and childbirth are a leading cause of death among women aged between 15 and 19 years in the developing countries.[6] Those who survive such complications may suffer from physical ill-effects for the rest of their lives. It is important to distinguish between younger and older adolescents when discussing the risks of pregnancy. For women aged 18 or 19 years the factor of age barely adds to the hazards of pregnancy. Pregnant women of any age require good obstetric and antenatal care, and nutrition. For women who become pregnant before they are 15, mortality is 60 per cent higher than for women in general. Mothers under 15 are 3.5 times more likely to die from toxaemia. Infant mortality is 2.4 times higher for babies born to mothers below 15 years, than for babies born to mothers in their early 20s[7]

Pregnancy and birth are areas of real interest for teenagers. Because of the health risks, they will be interested to know about pre-natal and post-natal care, pregnancy symptoms and testing, fetal growth and development, labour and delivery.

II. SEXUAL BEHAVIOURS

Sexual adjustment is part of a person's total development into a mature individual. Sexual maturity helps to bring out what is best, most generous and most constructive in an individual's life. Sex is a basic drive upon which both race preservation and personal happiness depend. If sexuality does not evolve properly, the whole process of growth and development is affected negatively. Excessive sex repression tends to impair freedom and the functioning of an individual, to the extent that mating and sexual satisfaction are not attained. On the other hand, too much sexual freedom can interfere with normal demonstrations of love and mating functions, to the degree that sexuality remains on an infantile level. Disturbances in sexual development can lead to personal and social maladjustments.[8]

Under this main category, the following topics are covered:

a) Sex drive or sexual feelings in childhood and adolescence

The sexual attitudes are formed from early childhood, although sexual urges and emotions do not become apparent until the age of puberty.[9] At this time, many changes occur among young boys and girls. In the male, puberty begins with the appearance of nocturnal emissions or wet dreams. At about this time, a young men begins to experience a distinct sexual urge or drive that is associated with his genitals. This heightened sexual excitability leads to masturbation. The sexual drive of a young woman, on the other hand, is less genital-specific, and she tends to associate sex with romantic situations. This awakened sexual drive among the youth, particularly young men, creates a certain restlessness so that the youth are often considered by their elders as being different and difficult. These are the first stirrings towards the youth's development of an independent personality and existence, which tend to be interpreted as an emotional withdrawal from home and family, and as an apparent failure to communicate with parents or elders and to understand them.

b) Pre-marital sex and teen-age pregnancies

Pre-marital sex has given rise to a range of alarming problems. Today's teenagers are very different from teenagers of 20 to 30 years ago, when adolescents were expected to remain chaste. Nowadays sexual activity has become more acceptable among the youth and the society in general. Girls and boys are reaching sexual maturity at an earlier age. Because of their early menarche, girls are able to conceive at a younger age. As sexual intercourse among adolescents in some countries become common, teenage pregnancies are on the increase.[10] Up to a certain extent, sexual permissiveness is encouraged by sexual messages conveyed through the mass media.

Teenage pregnancies pose many problems.[11] In many countries, pregnancy out of wedlock is not acceptable. Strong social pressure may lead to forced marriage or illegal abortion, and may also provoke the women to commit suicide. Illegitimate children may face the problem of social and legal discrimination as well as economic hardships. If marriage is forced on the mother, there is on the mother, there is a high probability of marriage failure. Another problem, particularly in the developing countries, is the high rate of school drop-out due to teenage pregnancies. When the educational attainment of women is so impaired, the low status of women is perpetuated from generation to generation. Their opportunities for employment are reduced and their continued dependence on others for their livelihood is reinforced. Another major drawback is seen in their reduced marriage prospects. In terms of health, early reproduction is more emotionally and physically taxing than one which begins late.

III. SEX ROLES

A study of sex roles is vital to achieving one of the objectives of family life education, that is, to enable the youth to understand and cope with changes in their own lives and in their society, as for example, the breaking down of traditional social structures and the changing roles of men and women. Studies on sex-role stereotypes indicate that men and women generally hold stereotypes of the typical characteristics of males and females: males are logical, dominant, independent, unemotional and aggressive; women are sensitive, emotional, nurturing, and are somewhat dependent and submissive.[12] It is unlikely that such personality characteristics are completely innate, because in some cultures the women are aggressive and dominant while the men are emotional and sensitive. If there are inherent pre-dispositions that are different for each sex, it appears that particular cultures accentuate some and mask others. Furthermore, literature and the mass media tend to create, reinforce and perpetuate many sex role differentiations. Many experts agree that the pressure, anxiety and confusion about male and female roles are core issues in most concerns related to sexuality. Male pressure to perform, female pressure to have children, male pressure to hide feelings female pressure to be sexually-appealing without being sexual, and so on are factors which influence the high incidence of unwanted pregnancy, divorce and sexual dissatisfaction.[13] Stereotyped sex roles hinder people from developing their natural abilities and personalities.

Topics on sex roles cover masculinity and femininity in different cultures, stereotypes and role expectations, and the contribution of society, schools and media to the creation and perpetuation of sex stereotypes.

IV. SEXUALLY TRANSMITTED DISEASES

Sexually transmitted diseases as a major topic in sex education has become more important due to the increased incidence of STDs, especially the dramatic rise in the incidence of AIDS.[14] The increased incidence of venereal disease is basically due to two factors. Firstly, homosexual sex before and outside marriage has become more common in some societies. Also common is sex between males. Secondly, the condom, which prevents the transmission of sexually transmitted diseases, is not as popular a method of contraception as it should be. STD education should address two areas: factual education and the inculcation of the right social attitudes.[15] Students need to understand that STD is not only a serious social problem, but more importantly, a critical medical problem which can be prevented and treated immediately. A study of STDs include the various types of STDs, their origin, symptoms, treatment, and prevention. They include the following:

Gonorrhea is the most common sexually transmitted disease. It is a contagious venereal infection caused by the Gonococcus in which there is a purulent inflammation of the mucous membrances of the genitourinary tract. The disease can cause sterility and death. It can be treated with high doces of penicillion.

Syphillis is an infectious, chronic, venereal disease caused by a spiral shaped organism called Treponema Pallidum. It was discovered in 1906. Syhillis may be transmitted from the mother to fetus during pregnancy and can cause deformity, blindness or death of the baby. Syphillis is usually cured with doses of penicillin.

Herpes is also a viral infection which usually occurs below the waist or on and around the genitals. It cannot be completely cured.

Acquired Immune Deficiency Syndrome (AIDS) was first identified in 1981. As of March 1, 1991 a total of 334, 216 cases of AIDS have been reported by more then 150 countries. It is a much feared worldwide epidemic that has no near-term medical solution. A WHO brochure describes AIDS as follows:

AIDS begins with a virus, a microscopic infectious agent. The AIDS virus is not like the viruses we usually talk about. The AIDS virus invades and destroys the cells in the body that are responsible for defending the body against disease. This leads to severe weakening of the body's natural defense system. Because of this action on the immune system, the AIDS virus is called the Human Immuno-deficiency Virus, or HIV. AIDS is the name given to the last stage of an infection with this virus, when the breakdown in the immune system leaves the body vulnerable to life-threatening infections and cancers. It is these diseases that result in death."

AIDS is caused by a newly recognized retrovirus called human immuno deficiency virus (HIV). The primary targets of HIV are T4 helper cells, a subpopulation of Iymphocytes that are essential to the body's defence against disease. HIV infects and kills T4 helper cells, thus disrupting communication within the cellular immune system and progressively disabling body's defence against disease.

At the present stage of the HIV pandemic, asymptomatic infection with HIV is far more common than is the disease AIDS. But HIV infection can progress and result in a wide range of adverse immunological and clinical conditions. Clinical classification of disease associated with HIV infection incudes AIDS-related complex (ARC), AIDS itself, and HIV neurological disease (including dementia).

References

1. International Planned Parenthood Federation. *Growing Up In a Changing World. Part One: Youth Organizations and Family Life Education: An Introduction* (London, IPPF, 1985)p.9
2. Population Education programme. *Human Sexuality and Reproduction Module IX* (Manila, Ministry of Education and Culture, 1978)p.5
3. Federation of family Planning Associations. *A Curriculum on Family Life Education for Youth Organizations.* (Malaysia, Federation of Family Planning Associations, 1985) p.65
4. Steven Bignell. *Family Life Education: Curriculum Guide.* (California, Network Publications, 1980)p.53.
5. International Planned Parenthood Federation. *Adolescent Fertility: Report of an International Consultation* (London,IPPF, 1984) p.8-9.
6. Ibid.,p.35.
7. Ibid.,p.35.
8. Population Education Program. *Teacher's Guide in population Education for Health Education* (Manila, Ministry of Education and Culture, 1981 p.1-24.
9. Ibid., p.20
10. Steven Bignell. *Sex Education: Teacher's Guide and Resource Manual* (California, Network Publications, 1982)p. 161.
11. International Planned Parenthood Federation. *Adolescent Fertility: Report of an International Consultation.* (London, IPPF, 1984) p.33.
12. Federation of family Planning Association. *A Curriculum on Family Life Education for Youth Organizations* (Malaysia, Federation of Family Planning Association, 1985)pp. 506-507.
13. Steven Bignell. *Family Life Education: Curriculum Guide.* (California, Network Publications, 1980)p.219.

14. International Planned Parenthood Federation. *Adolescent Fertility: Report of an International Consultation* (London IPPE, 1984) p.37

15. Steven Bignell. *Family Life Education: Curriculum Guide* (California, Network Publications, 1980) p. 243.

16. WHO. Guidelines for the Development of a National AIDS Prevention and Control Programme (Geneva, World Health Organisation, 1988)p.I.

MODULE 1

PHYSICAL ASPECTS

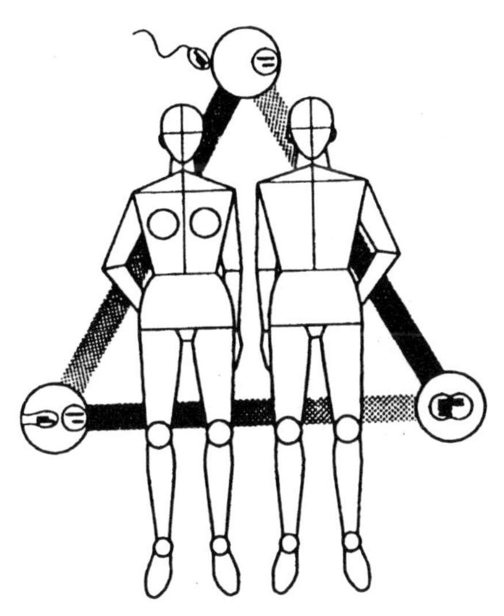

1

PHYSICAL ASPECTS

This is the first of a series of four modules that comprise a package entitled Adolescence Education. This module on physical aspects deals with the male and female reproductive systems; the physical, emotional and psychological changes that occur during puberty and the physiological processes of human conception. ?This particular module consists of the following lessons and their corresponding objectives:

Topics		Objectives
Lesson 1.1 Reproductive Systems Male and Female	(1)	To provide information about the male and female reproductive system
	(2)	To identify various parts of the male and female reproductive anatomy and their functions by locating corresponding parts of the body on diagrammes.
Lesson 1.2 Ovulation and Menstruation	(1)	To acquaint students with the process of ovulation and menstruation.
	(2)	To familiarize students with the terms used and the principles involved in this aspect of the female reproductive system.
Lesson 1.3 Physical, Emotional and Psychological Changes During Puberty	(1)	To enable students to understand and explore the range of physical, emotional and psychological changes during puberty.
	(2)	To differentiate the physical changes and characteristics of girls and boys.

Lesson 1.4 The Body Clock	To help the students become aware of the physical signs which indicate the reproductive maturity.
Lesson 1.5 Looking At Myself/ AS I see My Body	(1) To identify the adolescent's feelings about the various parts or aspects of their bodies. (2) To help the students increase their self-awareness and self-esteem by assessing theses parts of the body which they are satisfied with, and those parts which they would like to improve.
Lesson 1.6 Conception	To familiarize students with basic knowledge about the physiological processes of human conception
Lesson 1.7 Pregnancy and Essential Needs	(1) To provide the students with basic knowledge concerning the physiological processes in pregnancy (2) To make students aware of the signs and symptoms of pregnancy. (3) To make them understand the importance of antenatal care and essential needs during pregnancy.

Each lesson is provided with a set of objectives and indicates the time required for teaching, the materials to be used and the set of procedures to be followed in carrying out the teaching. Information sheets to help teachers in expanding the subject, reference materials and activities/exercises for students are also provided.

1.1 REPRODUCTIVE SYSTEMS:

Male and Female

Objectives :

(1) To provide information about the male and female reproductive systems.

(2) To identify various parts of the male and female reproductive anatomy and their functions by locating corresponding parts of the body on diagrammes.

Time Required : 80 minutes

Materials : Information Sheets and Worksheets

Worksheet 1.1.1 The Female reproductive system

Worksheet 1.1.2 The Female reproductive system (side view)

Worksheet 1.1.3 Female external genitalia

Worksheet 1.1.4 Male reproductive system (side view)

Worksheet 1.1.5 Bullbourethral glands and penis

PROCEDURE:

The purpose of this activity is to familiarize students with parts and functions of the male and female reproductive systems. Adolescents need this information in order to understand succeeding lessons concerning conception, pregnancy, contraception and pregnancy alternatives.

1. The teacher lists on the blackboard the names of the parts of the reproductive organs, as follows:

Female Reproductive System		*Male Reproductive System*	
Vulva	Cervix	Testicles or testes	Vas deferens
Mons pubic	Uterus	Penis	Seminal vesicle
Labia majora	Endometrium	Erection	Ejaculatory duct
Labia minora	Fallopian tubes	Semen	Prostrate gland
Clitoris	Ovaries	Scrotum	Cowper's gland
Urethra	Egg cells	Sperms	Urethra
Vagina	Progesterone	Testosterone	Bladder
Hymen	Estrogen	Androgens	
	Menstruation	Epidiymis	
	Bladder		

2. Prepare overhead transparencies or diagrammes of the male and female reproductive systems. Lecture on the various parts and functions of the male and female reproductive anatomy by using the following information sheet.

3. After the lecture, ask the students to identify the male and female organs by undertaking Activities 1.1.1, 1.1.2 and 1.1.4

INFORMATION SHEET

1. Male Reproductive system

The testicles or testes and the penis are the male external sex organs.

A) Penis

1. The penis is made up of spongy erectile tissue.
2. Most of the time it is soft and limp.
3. When a man becomes sexually excited, his penis stiffens and grows larger in width and length. When a man has strong sexual feelings, the blood flow out of the penis is slowed down and the spongy tissue of the penis fills with blood, causing the penis to become firm. This action is called an erection.

B) Testicles or testes

1. The testicles are two sex glands located in a wrinkled-looking pouch or sac called the scrotum, which hangs behind the penis.
   (a) Adult males have two testicles which are about the size and shape of plums.
   (b) The testicles contain hundreds of thousands of chambers where sperms develop.
   (c) The testicles correspond to the ovaries in women because both ovaries and testicles produce reproductive cells.
2. The scrotum controls the temperature of the testicles. Its temperature is about six degrees below body temperature. This is ideal for producing sperm.

C) Testosterone, androgens and sperm cells

1. One vital function of the testicles is hormone production. These male hormones are called androgens. Androgens are responsible for the physical development in males. Moreover they help activate male sexual behaviour.

2. The chief androgen produced in the testicles is testosterone. Messages from the pituitary gland signal the development of testosterone, the male sex hormone which prompts the production of sperms.

3. As sperms are produced, they pass through a very minor tube called the epididymis. While the sperms are resting in the epididymis, they mature until they are ready to be used. Then from the epididymis they pass through the vas deferens, on their way to the seminal vesicles. The seminal vesicles are small, sac-like structures which connect to the ejaculatory duct.

4. At the time of ejaculation, secretion from the two primary glands, the seminal vesicles and the prostrate are mixed with the sperm cells. The seminal vesicles empty some sugar into the vas deferens to provide energy for the sperms. The prostrate gland empties some milky fluid called semen into the ejaculatory duct to enable the sperms to swim easily. Two pea-sized bullbourethral glands or Cowper's glands also produce some fluid to cleanse the urethra of any urine residue which may prove harmful to the sperms.

   (a) Semen, or seminal fluid, is the whitish fluid that carries the sperm and is ejaculated during intercourse.

   (b) Each ejaculation contains 100 million to 600 million sperms in about a teaspoon of fluid.

5. From the ejaculatory duct, the sperms move through a long tube called the urethra through the penis. Both Urine and sperms are released from the body through the urethra. When the sperm is released, a valve closes off the flow of the urine.

6. Sperms

   (a) Sperms, which are miscroscopic male reproductive cells, make up less than two per cent of the total ejaculate.

   (b) They are much smaller than the egg.

   (c) They have a head and tail, resembling tadpoles.

(d) When ejaculated during sexual intercourse, they swim through the vagina, into the uterus through the cervix and on up into the fallopian tubes.

(e) Sperms can live for six to eight hours in the vagina.

(f) But once they get up into the uterus and tubes, they can live for three to five days.

(g) They usually reach the tubes within 1 to 1½ hours after ejaculating.

(h) Upon reaching the top of the uterus, half go into one fallopian tube and half go into the other.

(i) They swim against strong currents set up by the cilia in the fallopian tubes which act to draw the egg down toward the uterus.

(j) Of several hundred million sperms ejaculated, only abut 2,000 reach the tubes.

(k) Even though the egg must be totally surrounded by sperm in order to be fertilized, only one sperm is able to penetrate it. The rest are absorbed by the body.

(l) Sperm cells only retain the ability to fertilize an egg 48 to 72 hours.

II. FEMALE REPRODUCTIVE SYSTEM

A. Vulva

1. The female external reproductive organ or genitalia is called the vulva.

2. At the upper part is the mons pubis which is the fatty cushion situated at the pubic area where the pubic hair grows.

3. Below the mons pubis are two rounded folds of skin parallel to each other called labia majora or outer lips. Under the labia majora are the labia minora or the inner lips. The labia cover and protect the vaginal opening.

4. The clitoris is a small cylindrical body located in the soft folds in the upper part of the vulva. The clitoris is the

counterpart of the penis of the man. Because the clitoris comes from the same tissue that develops into the head of the penis in the male, it has the same nerve endings as the glands and because it is so much smaller, it is very sensitive.

5. Below the clitoris is the urethra, which is the passageway for urine from the bladder to the outside of a woman's body.

B. Vagina

1. Just below the urethral opening is the entrance to the vagina.

2. The vagina is the elastic muscular passage extending from the women's outer sexual organs (the vulva) to the uterus.

3. The vagina which is about four inches long is the female organ for sexual intercourse. It receives the penis during sexual intercourse.

4. Besides serving as organ for sexual intercourse, it also serves as the birth canal, the passage through which a baby is born.

5. The vagina is not a hollow tube. The walls are collapsed when empty; however, it can stretch to accommodate various sizes during birth, intercourse and menstruation.

6. The vagina is designed to clean itself by periodically shedding mucus and dead cells.

7. Oftentimes, but not always, there may be a small web of skin called the hymen partly covering the opening of the vagina.

C. Cervix

1. At the upper end of the vagina and the opening of the uterus is a button like structure called cervix.

2. The cervix is the entrance to the uterus and contains mucus producing glands.

3. The cervix feels like the end of a nose with a dimple in it.

4. If fertile mucus is present in the vagina during intercourse, sperm released by the male will travel through the cervical opening and into the uterus.

D. Uterus

1. The uterus, also known as the womb, is a pear-shaped muscular organ in which the fertilized egg grows and develops into a fetus.

2. Normally, the uterus is about three inches long and two inches wide. During pregnancy it stretches and grows with the fetus.

3. In pregnant women, the lining of the uterus, called the endometrium, nourishes the fetus.

4. In non-pregnant women, the lining is shed about once a month if an egg is not fertilized. This shedding is called menstruation.

E. Falloplan Tubes

1. The fallopian tubes are four to six inches long in a mature female. They curve around the ovaries and extend to the uterus. These tubes are the passageway through which the egg travels from the ovary to the uterus.

2. Each fallopian tube links one ovary with the uterus.

F. Ovaries

1. Connected by ligaments to the uterus are two ovaries: one on each side of the uterus.

2. These are the organs which store the egg cells. They also produce some of the female sex hormones which regulate the menstrual cycle and are responsible for the development of female secondary sex characteristics.

3. At birth, a girl's ovaries contain all the eggs she'll ever have—about 400,000. However, she'll probably use only about 400 of the eggs in her lifetime.

4. The ovaries produce a hormone called estrogen which is carried by the bloodstream to the uterus where it stimu-

lates the growth of the lining of the uterine wall called endometrium.

G. Eggs or Ova

1. Eggs or ova (which are about the size of a dot made by a sharp pencil) are some of the largest cells in the human body.
2. When the egg is expelled from the ovary, it travels to the uterus in one of the fallopian tubes. This takes between three to five days.
3. The egg cell dies if it is not fertilized within 12-24 hours after ovulation.
4. Fertilization occurs in the outer 1/3 of the fallopian tube.
5. If fertilization does not occur the egg cell will dissolve and be absorbed by the body.
6. After ovulation, the ovary secretes progresterone and also more estrogen.
7. The progesterone maintains the uterine lining.
8. If fertilization does not occur, the ovary will stop producing estrogen and progesterone after about two weeks.
9. This decline in hormones signals the uterus to shed its lining (menstruation).
10. If fertilization does occur, estrogen and progesterone continue to be produced and the uterine lining is not shed. This lack of a menstrual period is usually one of the first signs that pregnancy has occured.

H. Menstruation

1. Menstruation or periods come about once a month for most women.
2. Menstrual flow consists of blood, mucus and fragments of lining tissue. This flow gradually comes out of the uterus through the vagina. Shortly afterwards more egg follicles begin to develop, a new lining begins to build up and the cycle starts all over again.

3. Periods last three to seven days in most women, but this also varies.

4. At the onset, a woman's periods may be irregular—every three, four five or six weeks. Then gradually the body develops its own pattern of regularity.

5. Some women feel uncomfortable on the first or second day of their periods, but for most women menstruation does not interfere with their normal activity.

SUGGESTED ACTIVITY 1.1.1

Directions: On the blank sheet provided, write the letter corresponding to the definition of each of the organ of the male reproductive system.

(1) Male Reproductive Organs	(2) Definitions
1. Testicle/testis	A. Duct through which urine and semen are discharged.
2. Penis	B. Either of two ducts that allows sperms to pass from the testicle.
3. Scrotum	C. A rod which connects the vas deferens and the urethra.
4. Urethra	D. A filling station that provides the sperm with sugar energy.
5. Vas deferens	E. The gland in the male that produces - sperms
6. Seminal vesicle	F. The external pouch that contains the testicles.
7. Semen	G. The male sex organ; also the male urinary organ.
8. Sperm	H. A small tube like resting station on top of each testes where the sperms mature.
9. Testosterone	I. A gland in the brain that sends a message to the testicles to make sperms.
10. Androgens	j. A storage container for milky water which helps the sperms swim more easily.
11. Epididymis	K. A milky, sugary liquid containing the sperms which leaves the male body through the urethra in the penis.
12. Prostrate gland	L. The male reproductive cell made in the testicles.
13. Cowper's gland	M. The male sex hormone which prompts the production of sperm.
14. Ejaculatory duct	N. Gland that squirts out a cleansing fluid to clear the urethra.

15. Pituitary gland | O. Hormone which is responsible for physical development in males.

SUGGESTED ACTIVITY 1.1.2

Direction: Look at the diagramme below and write the correct name for each part

Male Reproductive System (Side View)

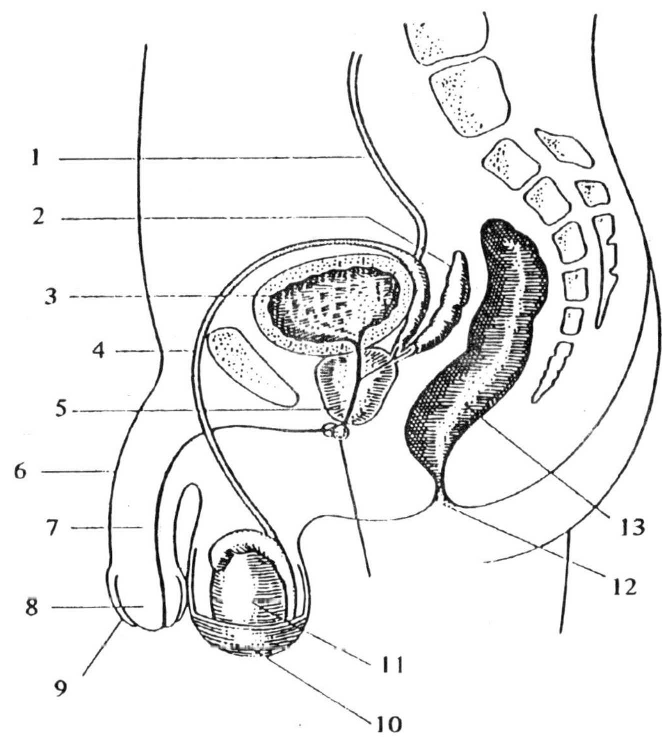

SUGGESTED ACTIVITY 1.1.3

Direction: On the blank sheet provided write the letter corresponding to the definition of each of the organ of the female reproductive system.

(1) Female Reproductive Organs	(2) Definitions
1. Vulva	A. Pear-shaped female reproductive organ in which the fetus grows and develops until birth.
2. Mons pubis	B. Female organ in which egg cells and sex hormones are produced.
3. Labia majora	C. Neck-like, narrow end of uterus which opens into vagina; it stretches to allow a baby to be born.
4. Labia minora	D. Either of two tubes through which egg released from an ovary every month travels to the uterus.
5. Clitoris	E. The passage that extends from the outer sexual organs to the uterus and is the organ for sexual intercourse.
6. Urethra	F. The external reproductive organ.
7. Vagina	G. Passageway of urine from the bladder.
8. Hymen	H. Fatty cushion at the upper part of the vulva situated at the pubic area where the pubic hair grows.
9. Cervix	I. The lining of the uterus which nourishes the foetus.
10. Uterus	J. Hormone which is carried to the uterus to stimulate the growth of the lining of the uterine wall called endometrium.
11. Endometrium	K. Hormone which maintains the uterine lining.
12. Fallopian tube	L. Outer lips of the vulva.
13. Ovary	M. Inner lips of the vulva.
14. Egg cell or ovum	N. Web of skin which partly covers the opening of the vagina.
15. Estrogen	O. Considered as the counterpart of the penis of the man, it is a small cyclindrical body located in the soft folds in the upper part of the vulva.
16. Progesterone	P. Female reproductive cell which is fertilized produces a baby.

SUGGESTED ACTIVITY 1.1.4

Direction: Look at the diagramme below and write the correct name for each part.

The Female Reproductive System

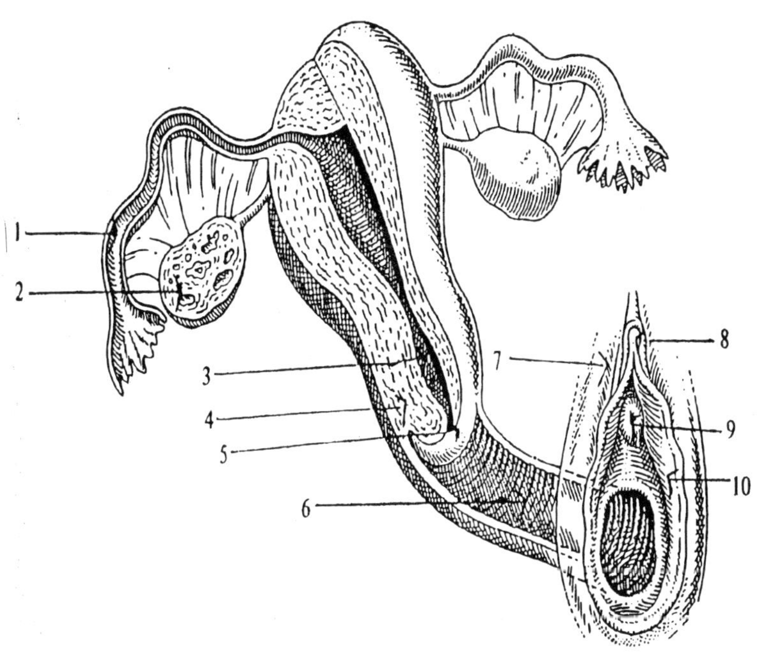

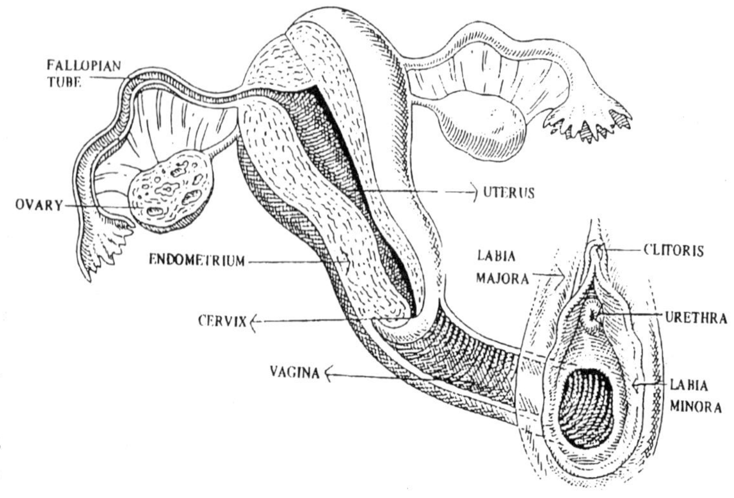

Worksheet 1.1.1 The Female Reproductive System

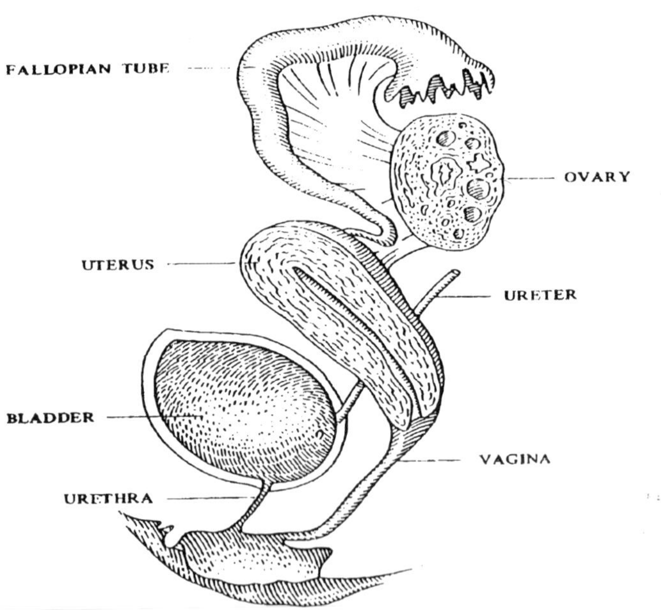

Worshieet 1.1.2 The Female Reproductive System: Side view

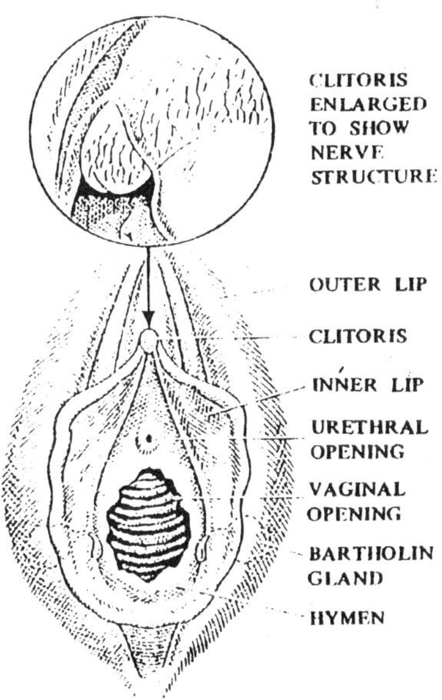

Worshieet 1.1.3 The Female External Genitalla

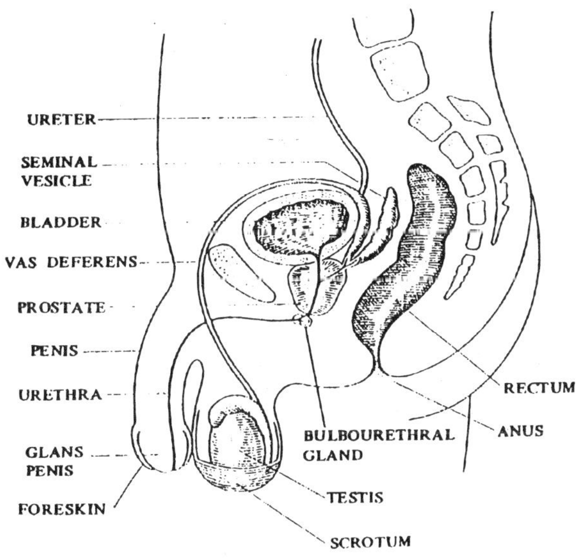

Worksheet 1.1.4 The Male Reproductive System: Side View

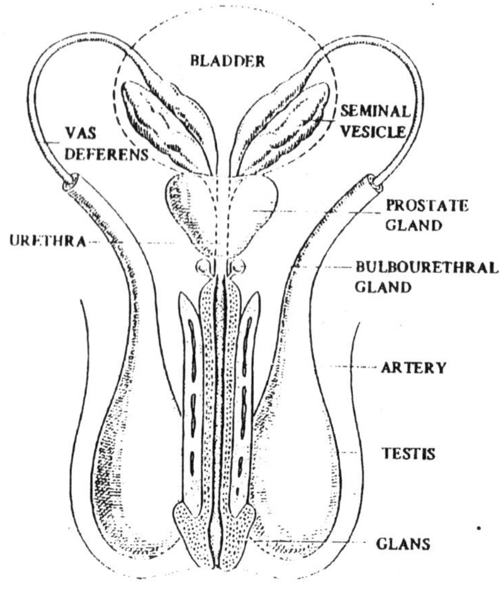

Worksheet 1.1.5 The Bullbourethral Glands and Penis

1.2 OVULATION AND MENSTRUATION

Objectives :

(1) To acquaint students with the process of ovulation and menstruation.

2) To familiarize them with the terms used and the principles involved in this aspect of the female reproductive system.

Time Required : 60 minutes

Materials : Information Sheets and Worksheets

Worksheet 1.2.1 Female reproductive system

Worksheet 1.2.2 Ovulation and menstruation

PROCEDURE

1. Present an introductory lecture on ovulation and men-

struation, referring to the information outline given in this lesson.

2. On an opaque projector display Worksheet 1.2.1, showing a frontal view of the female sex organ. Trace the path taken by the egg from the ovary, through the fallopian tubes, and into the uterus. Explain that if conception does not take place (if there is no sperm present to impregnate the egg), then the lining of the uterus sloughs off and is discharged through the vagina.

3. Duplicate and distribute Worksheet 1.2.2. Have the students follow your explanation on their diagrammes and repeat with you several times the path taken by the egg from the ovary to the uterus, as well as the subsequent occurrence of menstrual flow when conception does not take place.

   These facts deserve emphasis:

   a) The age at first menstruation varies widely. Each girl's body has its own time schedule for the changes of puberty.

   b) The first menstrual period usually follows other physical changes: growth spurt, breast development, body hair, etc.

   c) The beginning menstruation signals a girl's ability to get pregnant.

   d) During the first years, the menstrual cycle may have a very irregular frequency and duration.

   e) Blood is released slowly and flows gradually over a number of days.

   f) Mothers should prepare their daughter who have started physical development for their first menstrual periods. (In the absence of a mother, the school nurse or a trusted female adult should encourage the girls to talk to them, in case they are not comfortable in discussing the matter with their father).

   g) The first menstruation is called menarche. The final

disappearance of menstruation is called menopause.

4) After the lecture, have students carry out Suggested Activity.

COMMENTS AND CONSIDERATIONS

A number of concerns are likely to arise in connection with the topic of menstruation. Students may express concern about considerable blood loss, exercise, such as swimming, during menstruation, the use of sanitary napkin versus tampon (latest information about tampon use would be valuable to the students at this point), and body odor and the need to bathe or shower.

This may be presented in part or in its entirety before same-sex groups. Young people feel more free to ask questions about this topic when members of the opposite sex are not present.

INFORMATION SHEET

1. Teaching about ovulation and menstruation

A. The first menstruation is a big event in a young girl's life and it is anticipated with ambivalent feelings and expectations. Teachers can help make this event a positive experience by:

1. affirming the mother's role in the preparation for first menstruation. When there is no mother in the home, some fathers and daughters may be comfortable preparing for the first menstruation together. If this is not the case, encourage girls to seek out a trusted female adult or the school nurse to prepare for the first menstruation.

2. alleviating two major concerns: what to do if the period starts at school, and the fear that blood will 'gush out"

3. being sure school staff is prepared to give assistance to female students in a manner that will alleviate any embarrassment.

B. Discussing menstruation in class can be embarrassing for

girls if boys start teasing. Remind the class that a period is a normal function of a healthy female body. That it is a personal matter, and that teasing or joking about it is not acceptable mature behavior and that it shows lack of respect for other' feelings.

C. Male and female teachers often team up to present ovulation and menstruation topics. In this way, girls can discuss hygiene with a woman while the man has a separate class with the boys. Male teachers can be important role models for boys by approaching the subject of menstruation in a matter-offact and respectful way.

D. Parents and students may benefit from seeing a film about menstruation together. Your school might invite students and their parents to a special showing in the afternoon and/or evening. However, teachers need to be sensitive to students whose parents cannot attend such programmes by not overemphasizing their importance.

II. Ovulation

A. One of the things that happens during puberty is the production of hormones by the ovaries.

B. Estrogen is the female hormone that causes the changes during puberty: physical growth, development of the ovaries, breast development, body hair and body contours.

C. Each month an ovum (egg cell) matures and ripens.

D At the same time, the lining of the uterus (endometrium) builds up preparation for a fertilized egg.

E. The ovum takes a four to six day trip down the fallopian tubes in the uterus. Occasionally, two or more ova are released at the same time.

F. If the egg is not fertilized, the uterus will know that the endometrium is not needed.

III. Menstruation

A. Menstruation occurs when the lining of the uterus (the endometrium) begins to slough off the walls and slowly pass out of the body through the vagina.

B. The first menstruation usually comes between the ages of nine and 16, although it is normal to begin earlier or later. The first menstrual period is called menarche.

C. The first menstruation may begin before ovulation takes place (and ovulation may take place before the first menstruation).

D The menstrual flow is quite slow and gradual. The first sign of menstruation will be small spot of discharge, not a "gushing". (As mentioned earlier, the teacher should make a special effort to alleviate the common fear that a large amount of blood will gush out.)

E. The first periods are often very irregular. It is not uncommon to skip a month or to have periods close together.

F. Length of periods varies from two days to a week.

G. Gradually, a regular cycle will be established; but it's still quite normal and common during the teen years to have irregular periods.

IV. Preparation for menstruation

A. Soon after puberty begins, young girls and their mothers will need to get prepared for the first menstrual period.

B. In some homes, the first menstrual period is considered a special event deserving family celebration. In other homes, the event is quietly acknowledged by mother and daughter. However it is received, it marks the passage into womanhood.

1. Although for most there is a lapse of a few months to a year before conception can take place, some young women can conceive immediately. Others have conceived before the first menstrual period.

2. Being able to conceive does not mean readiness for parenting. In some cultures, parenting involves a great level of maturity and selfreliance.

C. Girls will want to discuss the different things they will need when their periods start. They"ll need to be prepared with sanitary pads or tampons and possibly a sanitary belt or special underwear. Sanitary pads or napkins are gauze-covered cotton pads worn during menstruation to absorb the flow of blood. They have a plastic layer on the underside to keep blood from coming through and staining clothes.

D. The class should understand how teachers and other adults at their school are ready to help girls if the need arises.

E. Menstrual blood has little odor and a daily both or shower will be sufficient to keep clean and smell fresh.

F. Some people feel uncomfortable just before and during their periods. There are some simple things that can help.

1. The body may retain more water at this time. Cutting down on salty foods will help prevent this.

2. Exercise speeds up circulation and helps case tension or headache. Exercise speeds up circulation and helps ease tension or headache. Exercise also relieves constipation which frequently increases the feelings of discomfort.

3. Drinking several glasses of water each day will aid digestion and lessen constipation.

4. Most girls will feel better if they get plenty of sleep during their period.

5. If girls do get cramps, there are several things they can do:

a. Place a hot water bottle on the abdomen(or on the back if that is where the cramps are).

b. Take a warm bath.

c. Drink a hot beverage (camomile, comfrey and /or rasberry leaf tea are sometimes suggested due to high calcium content and reported cramp relief).

d. Take a walk.

e. Rub or massage the abdomen (or ask someone to rub your back if it aches).

f. Get on elbows and knees so that the uterus is hanging down, which helps it relax.

g. Lie on the back with knees up, move the knees in small circles.

6. Most of all, since menstruation is natural and normal, girls should continue their usual routine unless it causes discomfort.

SUGGESTED ACTIVITY

Below are eight Illustrations describing the various stages of ovulation and menstruation. For each illustration or stage, write the corresponding description of events that occur.

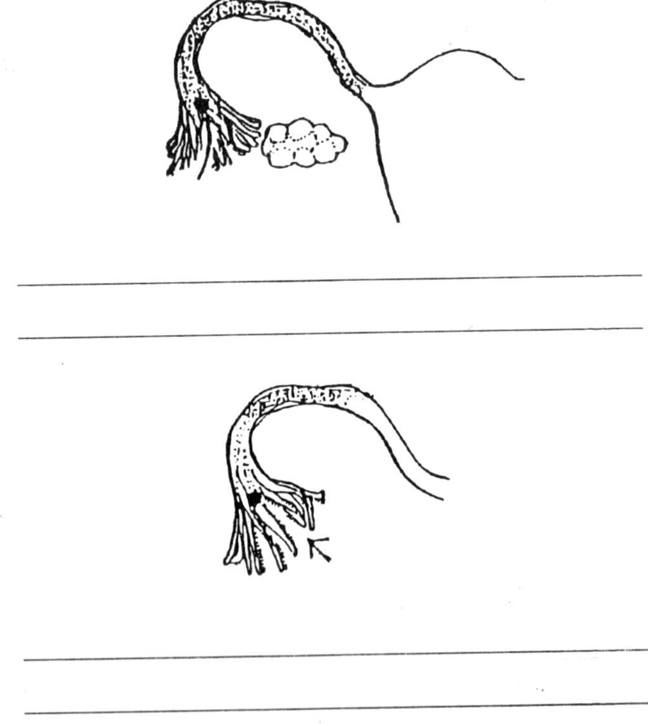

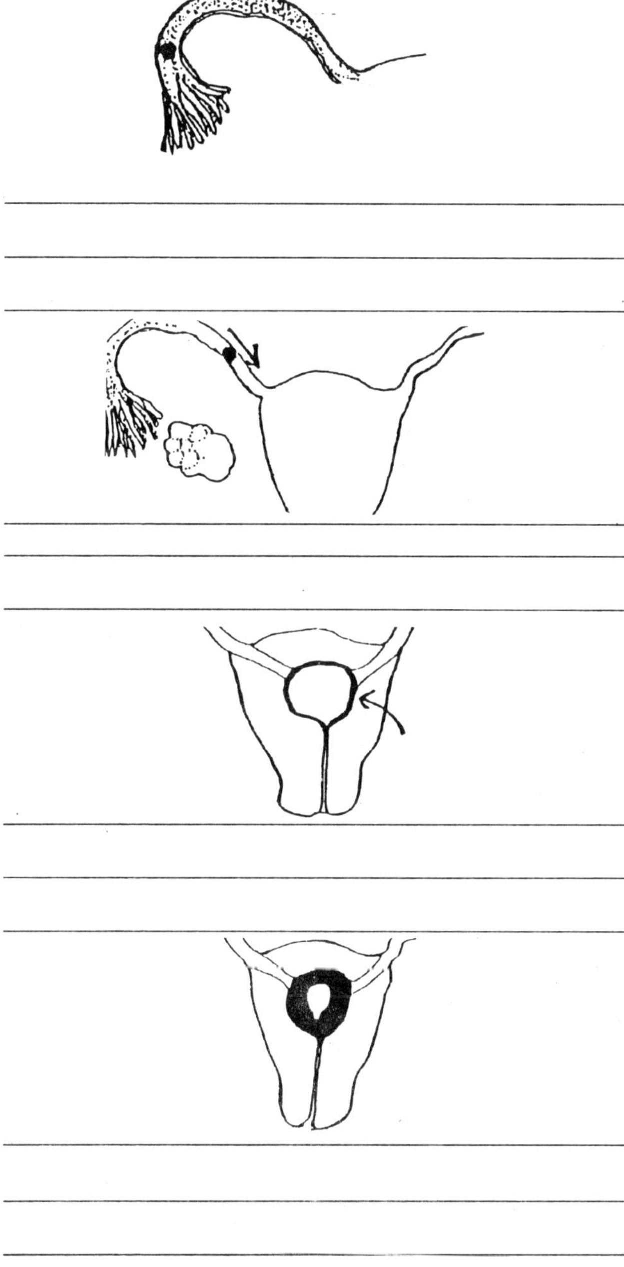

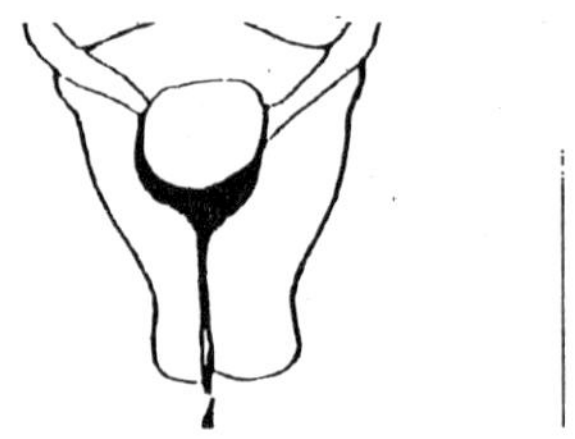

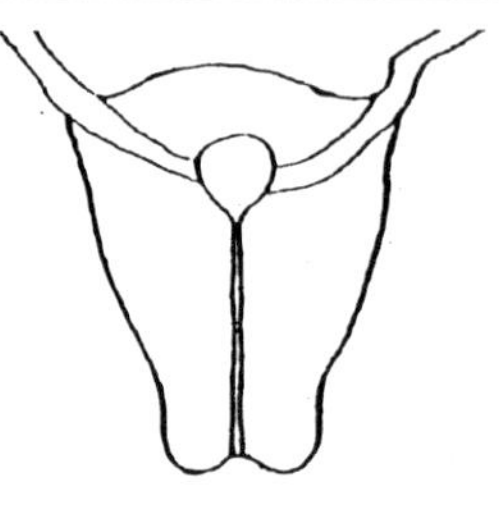

Worksheet 1.2.1 The Female Reproductive Organs

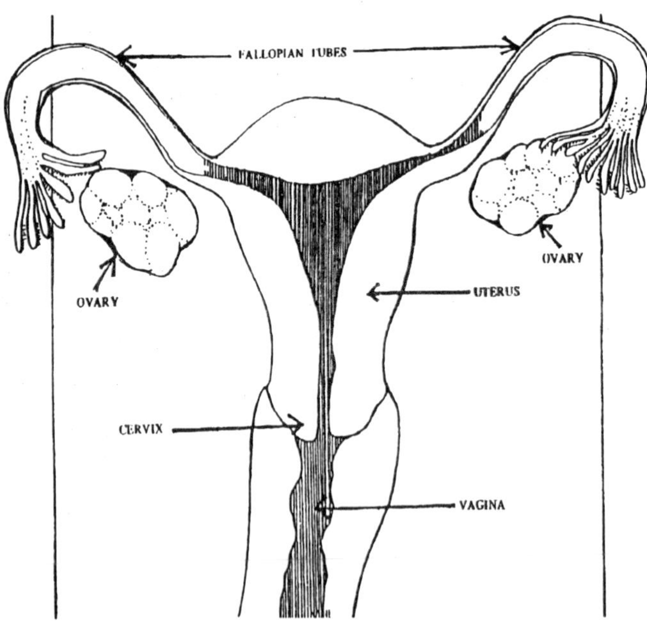

Worksheet 1.2.2 Ovulation and Menstruation

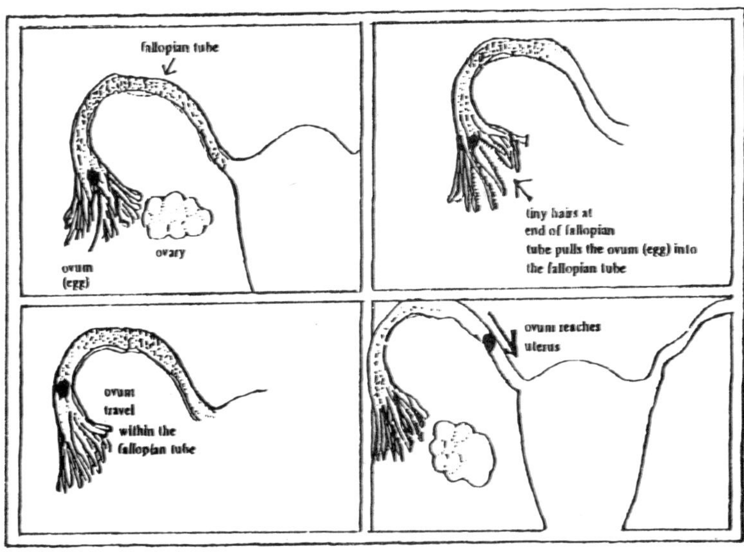

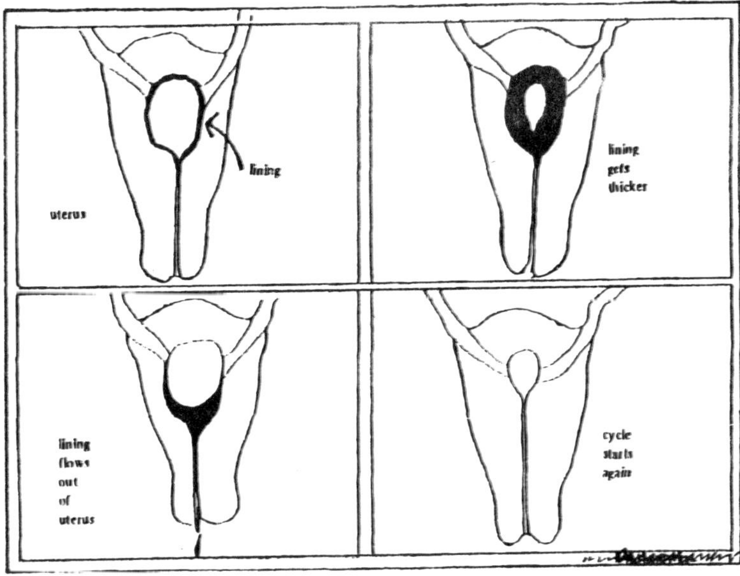

1.3 PHYSICAL, EMOTIONAL AND PSYCHOLOGICAL CHANGES DURING PUBERTY

Objectives :

1) To enable students to understand and explore the range of physical, emotional and psychological changes during puberty.

2) To differentiate the physical changes and characteristics of girls and boys.

Time Required: 60 minutes

Materials : Overhead projector, blackboard/whiteboard, chalk and duster/marker pen and duster, manila board/ blank transparency/mahjong paper as alternative to blackboard.

Worksheets and Information Sheets

Worksheet 1.3.1	Physical changes during adolescence
Worksheet 1.3.2	Sequence of events at adolescence in girls
Worksheet 1.3.3	Sequence of events at adolescence in boys
Worksheet 1.3.4	Strength of hand grip from age 11 to 17
Worksheet 1.3.5	Strength of arm pull and arm thrust from age 11 to 17
Worksheet 1.3.6	Physical changes of adolescent girls
Worksheet 1.3.7	Physical changes of adolescent boys

PROCEDURE

1. Ask the learners to list down the physical changes during adolescence for both girls and boys by undertaking Activity 1.3 A.1. Collect their listings and summarize the data on the board such as:

Physical changes during adolescence

Female changes	*Male changes*
Spurt in weight	Spurt in weight
Spurt in height	Spurt in height
Budding of breasts	Slight, temporary development of breasts around nipples
Growth of pubic hair	Growth of pubic hair
Growth of hair under arms	Growth of hair under arms
Deepening of voice	Voice change
Increase in perspiration	Increase in perspiration
	Growth of penis and testicles
Acne	Acne
Menarche (onset of menstruation)	Involuntary ejaculation
Widening of hips	Widening of chest and shoulders
Thighs become funnel-shapped	Arms become more muscular: Con siderable hardening of muscles.
	Heavy growth of hair on face and body.
Changes in body shape: from a slender child's body to that of an adult	Changes in body shape: from a slender child's body to that of an adult
	Increase in physical strength and stamina
Arrest of skeletal growth	Arrest of skeletal growth

Worksheets Nos. 1.3.1 to 1.3.7 can be used to help learners understand the differences in physical changes between male and female adolescents. It should be noted that girls develop a year or two ahead of the boys.

2. Show the worksheets and ask the learners to compare the list of changes which they have compiled with the changes shown on the worksheets.

3. Pick up a few problems for discussion. (This activity is only for those trainers who have the capability or expertise on the subject matter selected).

4. Ask the learners to accomplish Activity 1.3.2.

SUGGESTED ACTIVITY 1.3.1

Instructions:

1. List all the physical changes which the adolescent boys and girls encounter.

2. Place a tick (..) in the column "Myself" if you had similar encounters.

Female	*Male*	*Myself*

SUGGESTED ACTIVITY 1.3.2

Instructions:

1. Complete the sentences which bring out the most conscious and problematic changes that adolescents undergo.
2. Do NOT write your name on the paper.

1. The physical changes during adolescence which I was (or am) MOST CONSCIOUS of is

____

____

____

____

____

____

____

because _______________________________________

____

____

2. The physical change during adolescence which was (or is) MOST PROBLEMATIC for me is

____

____

because ____

WORKSHEET 1.3.1. PHYSICAL CHANGES DURING ADOLESCENCE

Female	*Male*
Spurt in weight	Spurt in weight
Spurt in height	Spurt in height
Budding of breasts	Slight temporary development of breasts around nipples
Growth of pubic hair	Growth of pubic hair
Growth of hair under arms	Growth of hair under arms
Change of voice	Deepening of voice
Increase in perspiration	Increase in perspiration
	Growth of penis and testicles
Appearance of Acne	Appearance of acne
Menarche (onset of menstruation)	Involuntary ejaculation
Widening of hips	Widening of chest and shoulders
Thighs become funnel-shaped	Arms becoming more muscular
	Considerable hardening of body muscles
	Heavy growth of hair on face and body
Changes in body shape: from the slenderness of a child's body to that of an adult	Changes in body shape: from the slenderness of a child's body to that of an adult
	Increase in physical strength and stamina
Arrest of skeletal growth	Arrest of skeletal growth

WORKSHEET 1.3.2 SEQUENCE OF EVENTS AT ADOLESCENCE IN GIRLS

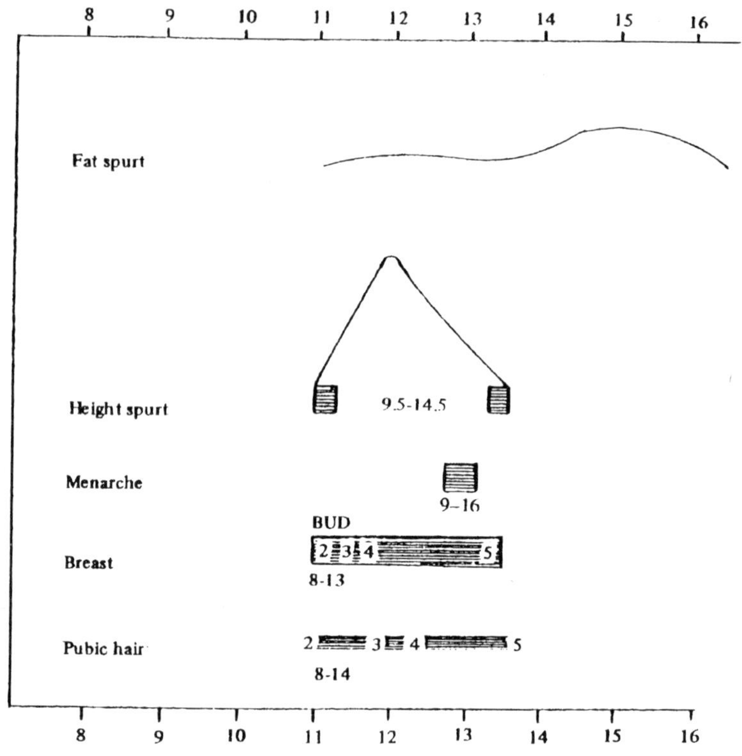

Age in Years

Diagramme showing the sequence of events at adolescence in average girls. The range of ages within which some of the events occur is given by the figures (appropriate to 1955) placed directly below them.

WORKSHEET 1.3.3 SEQUENCE OF EVENTS AT ADOLESCENCE IN BOYS

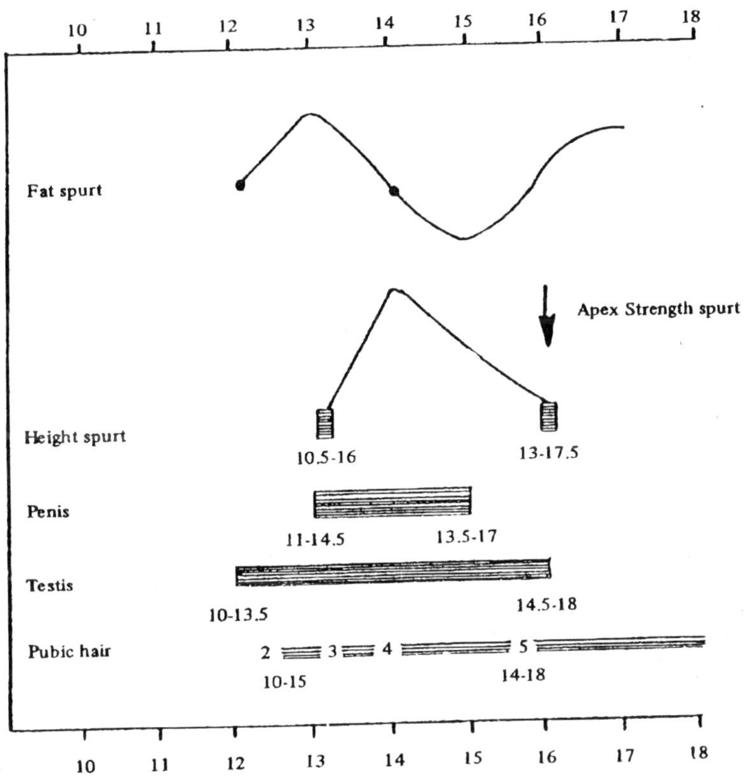

Age in Years

Diagramme showing the sequence of events at adolescence in average boys. The range of ages within which each events charted may begin and end is given by the figures (appropriate to 1955) placed directly below them.

Worksheet 1.3.4 Strength of Hand Grip from Age 11 to 17 Year

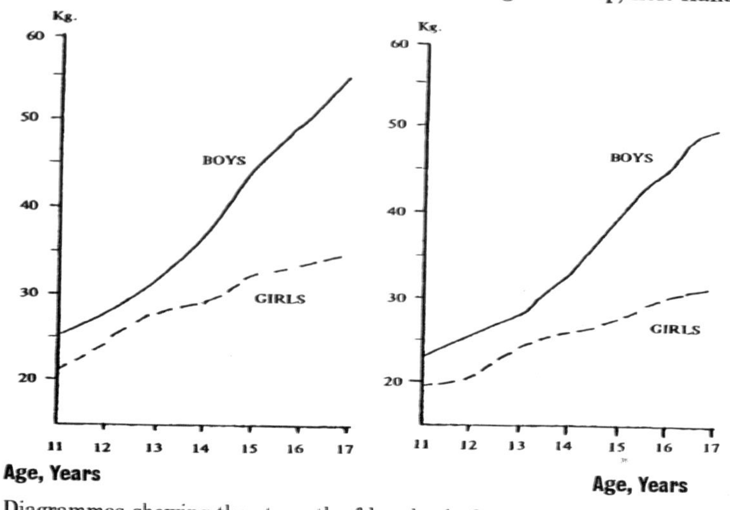

Diagrammes showing the strength of hand grip from age 11 to 17 of average boys and girls. Mixed longitudinal data where 65-93 boys and 66-93 girls in each group were used.

Worksheet 1.3.5 Strength of Arm Pull and Arm Thrust from age 11 to 17 Years

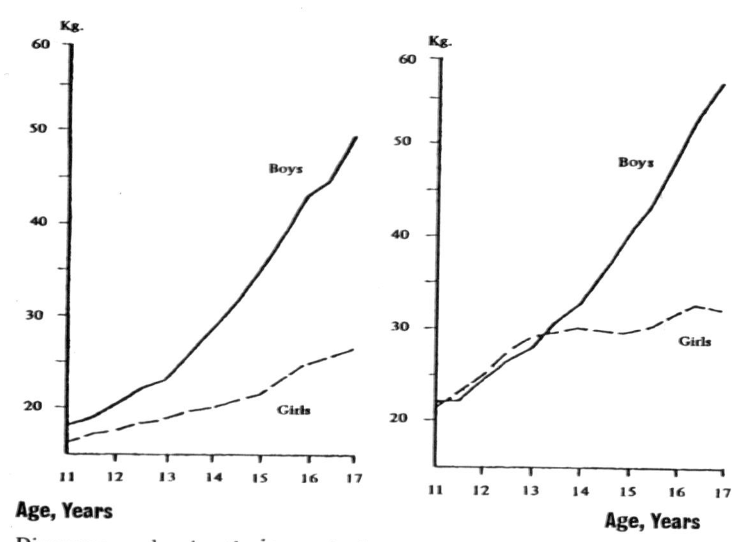

Diagrammes showing the strength of arm pull and arm thrust among boys and girls of average age 11 to 17. Mixed longitudinal data where 65-93 boys and 66-93 girls in each group where used. Data from Jones, Motor Performance and Growth, Univ. Calif. Press. 1949.

WORKSHEET 1.3.6 PHYSICAL CHANGES OF ADOLESCENT GIRLS

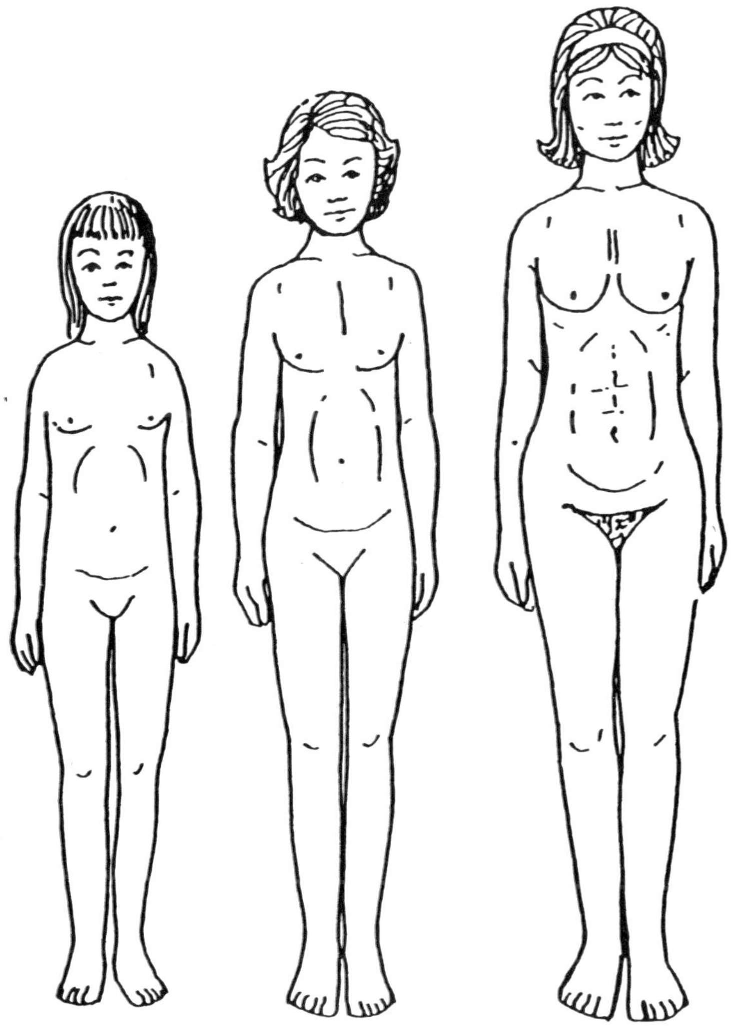

Can you identify the differences in the above three developmental stages of the girls?

WORKSHEET 1.3.7 PHYSICAL CHANGES OF ADOLESCENT BOYS

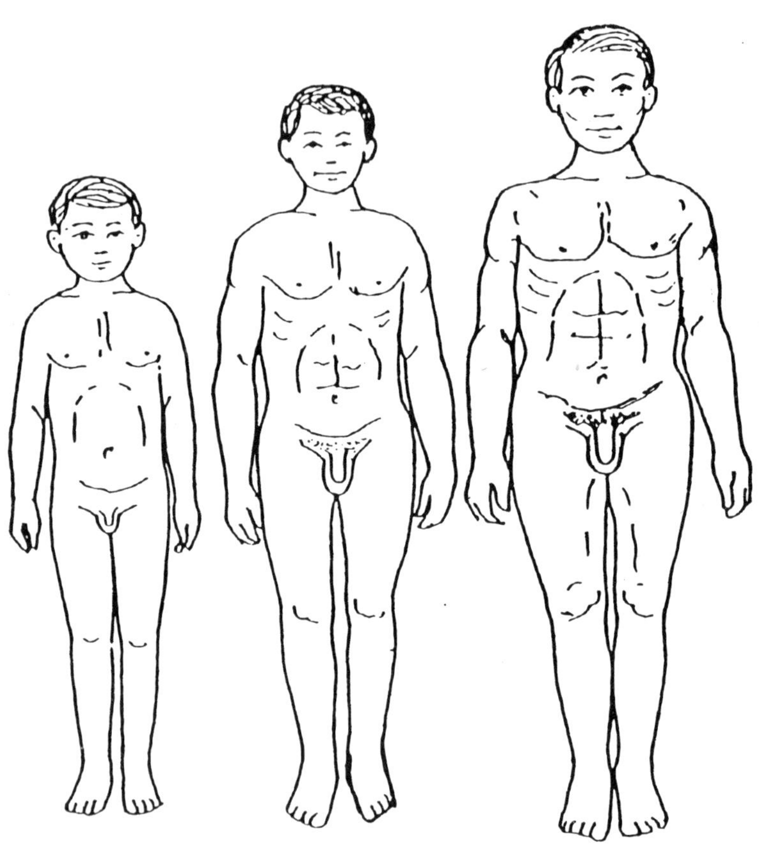

Can you identify the differences in the above three development stages of the boys?

1.4 THE BODY CLOCK

Objective :

To help the students be aware of the physical signs which indicate the reproductive maturity.

Time required : 80 minutes

Materials : Information Sheets and Worksheets

Worksheet	1.4.1	The female body clock
Worksheet	1.4.2	The male body clock

PROCEDURE

1. Discuss the sequence of physical changes for both male and female during puberty as well as the emotional changes that occur during this stage.
2. After the lecture, give each student a copy of the work sheets 1.4.1 and 1.4.2 " The Body Clock" (use the corresponding sheets for each sex). Tell the students to indicate the order in which they think the changes will occur by placing the numbers 1 to 8 in the circles.
3. After completing the Body Clock, ask the students to undertake another activity that will Enable them to differentiate between the physical and emotional changes of boys and girls (see suggested activity 1.4.1)
4. Finally, ask the students to identify the different developmental stages of adolescence and the behavioural tendencies that occur in each stage (see suggested activity 1.4.2)

Considerations In Teaching: At times most people wonder what the future holds for them. Since children know that many changes will occur during adolescence, it is easy to understand why they may be anxious to know how and when these events will take place. Girls frequently ask, "How will I know when my periods are about to begin?" Boys wonder if they will ever grow taller than girls. During puberty boys may also become needlessly worried about penis size.

Certainly teachers cannot predict an exact schedule for the individual child, but is is essential to provide reassurance by giving students information regarding the sequence of pubertal changes.

The onset of puberty can vary widely (for boys 10 to 14, for girls 8 to 12); however, the order in which the changes take place is generally the same. The developments happen in the following order:

Female Body Clock

1. Breast budding
2. Growth of bony pelvis
3. Growth spurt
4. Growth of pubic hair
5. First menstruation (menarche)
6. Growth of underarm and coarser body hair
7. Oil and sweat glands activated
8. Growth of uterus and vagina completed

Male Body Clock

1. Growth of testes and scrotum
2. Growth of straight pubic hair
3. First ejaculation
4. Growth spurt-arms, legs, and penis
5. Voice change- (Growth of larynx)
6. Growth of underarm and coarser body hair
7. Oil and sweat glands activated
8. Appearance of facial hair (Beard)

The "Body Clock" activity can help students be aware of the physical signs which indicate that most young people are reaching reproductive maturity on schedule. The "Body Clock" diagramme simplifies this process, but it does not indicate some of the more subtle changes which the teacher may want to explain. For example, pubic hair appears in two stages. The first growth which develops is straight and pigmented, at a later time the characteristically kinky type begins to grow. For girls the kinky pubic hair appears after the period of maximum growth and is the sign that first menstruation is approximately six months to a year away. For boys the straight pubic hair appears after the period of maximum growth and is the sign that first menstruation is approximately six months to a year away. For boys the straight pubic hair appears before the first ejaculation, but becomes kinky after this milestone is reached.

Voice changes for the male also take place in two stages. Some early voice changes occur prior to the first ejaculation, but the deep tonal transition comes after the appearance of axillary hair and the period of maximum growth. Boys may be relieved to learn that the beard really is the last thing to grow.

In addition to explaining some of these more subtle developments, the teacher also needs to point out that stages of development may not be as easily recognized in real life as they are on the "Body Clock" diagramme. Sometimes initial changes in body size or shape may be so slight that they go unnoticed. A girl may recognize that her hips are getting rounder about the same time that she first notices any changes in her breasts, even though breast development does occur first. For others the appearance of pubic hair may be the first observed signal of "growing up" even though a girl's breasts or a boy's testes have already increased somewhat in size. The "Body Clock" activity is designed to help young people know what signs to look for first, and to reassure those who are expecting all these changes to take place at the same time.

INFORMATION SHEET

The Female Body Clock

1. Puberty

   A. **Begins between ages of 8 to 12 and ends around age 16 or so.**

1. It take approximately 3-5 years to complete this stage of growth.
2. Onset of puberty is consistently 2 years earlier in girls than in boys. Girls reach full height about 2 years earlier than boys.
3. Females are born with slightly more mature skeletons and nervous systems and gradually increase this development lead throughout childhood.
4. Earlier sexual maturation of females is one reason why males are about 10 per cent taller as adults; by virture of maturing later, males have more time to continue growing.
5. Biological changes vary in time of onset and duration, yet these changes fall into definite and predictable patterns.

II. SEQUENCE OF CHANGES

A. Breast Budding (first change)

1. This starts between ages of 8 and 13 (average age of 11).
2. This development is completed between ages of 13 and 18 (average age 15)
3. This hold a psychological importance to young female who may worry about its size and shape
   a. It is not unusual for one breast to develop faster than the other;
   b. An adolescent girl may worry about the asymmetry that results, especially if she doesn't know that the difference is usually corrected by the time development is completed;
   c. A certain amount of preoccupation and selfconsciousness is quite common.

B. Growth of Bony Pelvis (second change)

1. Girls at birth already have a wider pelvic outlet so that the natural adaptation for child-bearing is present from a very early age.

2. This change primarily involves the widening of the pelvic inlet and broadening the much more noticeable hips.

C. Growth Spurt (third change)

1. This usually starts at about age 10 1/2 (may begin as early as 9.5 years) and peaks at age 12:

   a. Growth spurt usually ends at around age 14;

   b. Any further noticeable growth in stature stops at age 18;

   c. At the end of the growth spurt, the average girl of 14 has already reached 98 per cent of her adult height.

2. The first menstrual period invariably occurs after peak height velocity is passed (usually 1 year), so that a girl can be reassured about future growth if her periods have begun.

3. The growth of legs and arms is not uniform:

   a. Usually the more distal parts of the limbs (feet and hands) grow faster first;

   b. This accounts for the gangly and awkward appearance of adolescents;

      ex: foot accelerates first followed by calf and thigh

      ex: hands, forearms, followed by upper arms

D. Pubic Hair (fourth change)

1. Pubic hair begins to grow between the ages of 11 and 12 (11.6—14.4) on the average.

2. The growth is completed by age 14:

   a. Kinky pubic hair appears after the period of maximum growth in height;

   b. This development is a sign that first menstruation is approximately 6 months to 1 year away.

3. Axillary hair appears on the average some 2 years after the beginning of pubic hair growth.

E. First Menstrual Period or Menarche (fifth change)

1. One lingering misconception—many people think menstruation marks the beginning of puberty when actually it is one of the later events to characterize this stage of life.

2. Generally age range for menarche may vary from 9-18 years.

3. This usually begins 2 years after the start of breast development (occurs after peak of growth spurt in height).

4. First menstrual cycles may be more irregular than later ones.

5. There may be a lag in time of 1 year to 18 months before ovulation becomes well established (however, this cannot be relied upon the individual case).

6. The present trend shows that:

   a. Successive generations have been generally getting taller and attaining puberty at progressively earlier ages;

   b. There is a declining age of menarche i.e, 4 months per decade;

   c. While in 1900, the average age for first menstrual period was 14 years, today the average age is 12.8 years—a development which is attributed to factors such as better nutrition and health.

F. Underarm Hair and Coarser Body Hair (sixth change)

While this development is expected, the ultimate amount of body hair an individual develops seems to depend largely on heredity.

G. Oil and Sweat Producing Glands (seventh change)

The activation of glands cause the following:

1. Appearance of acne;

2. Body odor.

H. Completion of the Growth of Uterus and Vagina (eighth change)

1. Although these starts developing early, their growth is the last to be completed.

2. The musculature wall of the uterus becomes larger and elaborate:

   a. This is designed to accommodate foetus during pregnancy as well as to expel it during childbirth;

   b. Cyclical changes occur in its lining (endometrium).

3. The vagina becomes larger and its lining grows thicker.

4. Vaginal contents, which are alkaline at the beginning of puberty become acidic at this stage.

5. At birth, the ovaries is a fairly complete organ:

   a. It contains about half a million immature ova—each one capable of becoming a mature egg;

   b. The female is born with all of the eggs which she is going to develop—usually 400 eggs;

   c. These follicles remain immature until puberty when ovulation begins;

   d. At puberty, the follicles start maturing into eggs in monthly cycles.

THE MALE BODY CLOCK

1. Puberty

Sequence of pubertal maturation is predictable, but the rate at which the events occur is highly variable. Generally, the onset of puberty begins between the ages of 10 or 11.

1. Onset of puberty is consistently 2 years later in boys than in girls.

2. Onset of puberty ranges from age 10 to 14.

3. Girls reach full height about 2 years before boys.

4. In the year in which a boy grows the fastest he normally adds 3 to 5 inches to his height.

5. An average boy of 16 has already reached 98 per cent of adult height.

II. SEQUENCE OF CHANGES

A. Growth of Testes and Scrotum (first change)

1. Onset of puberty is marked by the initial enlargement of the testes.

2. Growth of testes and scrotum usually begins between the ages of 10 and 13 1/2 years.

3. Development remains in progress through most of puberty and is completed sometime between the ages of 14 1/2 to 18 years.

4. Along with increasing growth of the testicles, reddening and wrinkling of scrotal skin occurs.

5. Testes are the male reproductive glands that produce sperm and the male hormones:

    a. Unlike ovaries, the testes do not contain all the sperms that will be produced;

    b. Testes are a conglomerate of solid threadlike cords called "seminiferous tubules";

    c. During puberty, these tubules increase in size and the cells in the lining of the tubules pass through a succession of stages;

    d. From puberty on, the testes continuously produce sperm generating billions in the course of an adult lifetime;

    e. Unlike ovaries, decline in testicular function is far more gradual than ovaries in terms of both sperm and hormone production.

B. Straight Pubic Hairs (second change)

1. Usually an early event of puberty, this occurs between

the ages of 10 and 15.

2. A prepubescent boy may have some finely textured hair but no true pubic hair.

3. Later, long strands of slightly curly hair appear at the base of the penis.

4. Pubic hair becomes darker, coarser, and more curly as it spreads over the scrotum and higher up the abdomen.

5. Straight pubic hair appears before the first ejaculation, but pubic hair becomes kinky after this milestone is reached.

C. First Ejaculation (third change)

1. This usually occurs about a year after testicular growth.

2. The average age for first ejaculation is 14.6 years of age.

D. Growth Spurt—arms, legs, penis (fourth change)

1. The start of penis growth spurt occurs normally between the ages of 10.5 5 and 14.5 years (average age 12.5):

   a. Age for completion of this growth spurt ranges from 12.5 to 16.5 years (average age 14.5);

   b. A late developer may begin to wonder whether he will ever develop his body properly or be as well endowed sexually as others.

2. Height spurt occurs relatively later in boys than in girls between ages of 11 and 13 years.

3. Average age for increase in height is age 14.

4. A short adolescent male whose genitalia are beginning to develop can be reassured that an acceleration in height is soon to take place.

5. In the year in which a boy grows the fastest, he normally adds from about 3 to 5 inches to his height.

6. The legs as a rule reaches its peak growth first.

7. The spurt in trunk length follows almost a year later.

8. Leg growth itself is not uniform. The foot accelerates first followed by the calf and thigh (more distal parts of the limbs grow faster first).

E. Voice Change—growth of larynx (fifth change)

1. Deepening of the voice results from the enlargement of the larynx.
2. This occurs relatively late in adolescence and often a gradual process.
3. Voice change undergo two stages:
    a. Some early voice change occur prior to the first ejaculation;
    b. Transition into a deep tonal voice comes after the appearance of axillary hair and the period of maximum growth.

F. Underarm and Coarser Body Hair (sixth change)

1. These generally appear a couple of years after the growth of pubic hair.
2. This change is accompanied by increased body and facial hair.

G. Oil and Sweat Glands Activated (seventh change)

1. Body odor develops with this occurrence.
2. Appearance of acne is also a result of this:
    a. Body odor and acne are common concerns for many adolescents;
    b. Increased production of androgen hormones accompanying puberty in both sexes leads to an increase in skin thickness and stimulates the growth of sebaceous glands (small glands in the skin which produce oil);
    c. Often these small glands grow more rapidly than the ducts that lead to the surface of the skin resulting in clogged pores, inflammation, and infection with the appearance of blackheads and pimples.

H. Facial Hair- Beard (eighth change)

1. This is an important event because of its social implications as a symbol or badge of manhood.

2. Facial hair begins to grow at about the time the axillary hair appears.

3. There is a definite order in which the hairs (moustache and beard) appear:

   a. The first facial hair to grow is that at the corners of the upper lip;

   b. Then it spreads to form a mustache over the entire upper lip;

   c. This is followed by the appearance on the upper part of the cheeks and the area under the lower lip;

   d. It eventually spreads to the sides and lower border of the chin and the rest of the lower face.

EMOTIONAL CHANGES FOR BOTH BOYS AND GIRLS

A. Increased production of hormones prompts sexual thoughts and daydreams in most young people; there is a heightened awareness of sexual attraction.

1. Release of semen by boys during sleep, called nocturnal emission or "wet dreams," is common at this time. It is also quite normal not to experience them.

2. Both boys and girls may experience sexual excitement from simply watching or being near someone they are attracted to. They may not understand that the emotions they are feeling are sexual in nature.

3. Sexual fantasies are common at this time:

   a. Some parents feel that this is a natural stage of development and not a matter of concern;

   b. Other parents feel that some daydreams or fantasies are not wrong but others are; and like various facets of human behavior, some fantasies need to be controlled.

4. In general, boys and girls become more interested in each other during puberty.

5. While sexual interest and thoughts are common, it is also quite normal not to be sexually concerned, especially in the early years of puberty.

B. Puberty is a time of frequent shifts of moods for most adolescents.

1. Discomfort and concern about the changes in their bodies and feelings may cause emotional stress.

2. Moods shift quickly and unpredictably.

3. Crying over seemingly small matters is common for both boys and girls and is not something to be ashamed of.

4. It helps young people to share their concerns with parents or friends. Often, they find comfort in discovering that others share similar concerns and feelings.

C. Increased feelings of independence are a part of the normal development in adolescence.

1. Adolescents experience frequent shifts of behaviour from mature to childish behavior.

2. Relationships with parents begin to change as young people assert their independence, sometimes causing difficulties.

DEVELOPMENTAL TASKS

Independence: Adolescents need to become less dependent on parents. They begin to shift from parents to peers or to belief systems in order to achieve independence. This shift is strong and may involve rebellion.

Identity: Adolescents struggle to define themselves and what they want to accomplish. They are answering the questions: "Who am I? What can I be?" This process involves experimenting. Adolescents need to develop gender role identity, a positive body image, and a sense of esteem and competence.

Intimacy: Adolescence is a time of preparation for loving relationships. Adolescents are learning to express and manage emotions. They are developing the capacity to love and be loved, and to be intimate in relationships with others.

Integrity: Adolescents must develop a foundation for sorting out values. Parents have provided a base for this. However, there is is a tremendous amount of other input at this time—peers, media, school, etc. Adolescents are deciding what to believe in and how to behave.

Intellect: The adolescent's intellectual capacity is increasing and changing from concrete thinking to include abstract thinking. Many adolescents become capable of conceptual thinking and of understanding logic and deductive reasoning. This increased ability may adolescents become capable of conceptual thinking and of understanding may heighten self esteem. Some adolescents tend to overvalue their intellectual theories and see things from an idealistic point of view.

DEVELOPMENT STAGES

The developmental stages manifest general tendencies but they do not necessarily describe a particular child. The stages may overlap.

Early adolescence: Onset of puberty, female ages 8-12; male ages 10-14.

Starts to move to peers
Vacillates between clinging and rebellion
Strives for independence
May be confused, preoccupied with body, wonder "am I normal"?
May experiment with same-sex sexual behavior
Beings to think abstractly

Middle adolescence: Female ages 13-16, male ages 14-17 (defined by peer group).

Continues effort to establish separate identity from parents
Often becomes idealistic and altruistic
Interested in dating, exploring sex
Loves intensely, "desperately"
Continues to develop abstract thinking

Late adolescence: Female ages 16 and over, male ages 17 and over.

Declares independence
Establishes a set body image
Loves more realistically, develops commitment
Peer group becomes less important, more selective of friend
Develops more consistent framework of values, morals, ethics
Able to think abstractly
Defines life goals

SUGGESTED ACTIVITY 1.4.1

Directions: On the spaces provided in the left-hand column, write your answers by identifying the gender to which the occurrence happens, i.e. M(Male) or F (Female) or B (Both) and whether the occurrence takes place during puberty (2nd column). Fill up the first column only if the second column is answered with a "yes".

To Whom	Yes Or No	
		1. Hormone action increases, bringing about body changes.
		2. Rapid changes in height and weight take place.
		3. Voices get higher.
		4. Growth of body hair begins.
		5. Breasts develop.
		6. Sweat glands are no longer active
		7. Shoulders widen.
		8. The reproductive organs begin to function.
		9. Nocturnal emissions are common.
		10. Menstruation begins.
		11. Changes in mood take place more often.
		12. Girls and boys are less interested in each other.
		13. There is an increased feeling of independence.
		14. Interests and friendships change.

SUGGESTED ACTIVITY 1.4.2

Direction: Write the various behavioural changes that occur under each adolescent stage.

I. Early onset of puberty, female ages 8-12, male ages 10-14

1.

2.

3.

4.

5.

6.

II. Middle: Female ages 13-16 male ages 14-17

1.

2.

3.

4.

5.

III. Late: Females ages 16 and older and male ages 17 and older

1.

2.

3.

4.

5.

6.

7.

Worksheet 1.4.1 The Female Body Clock

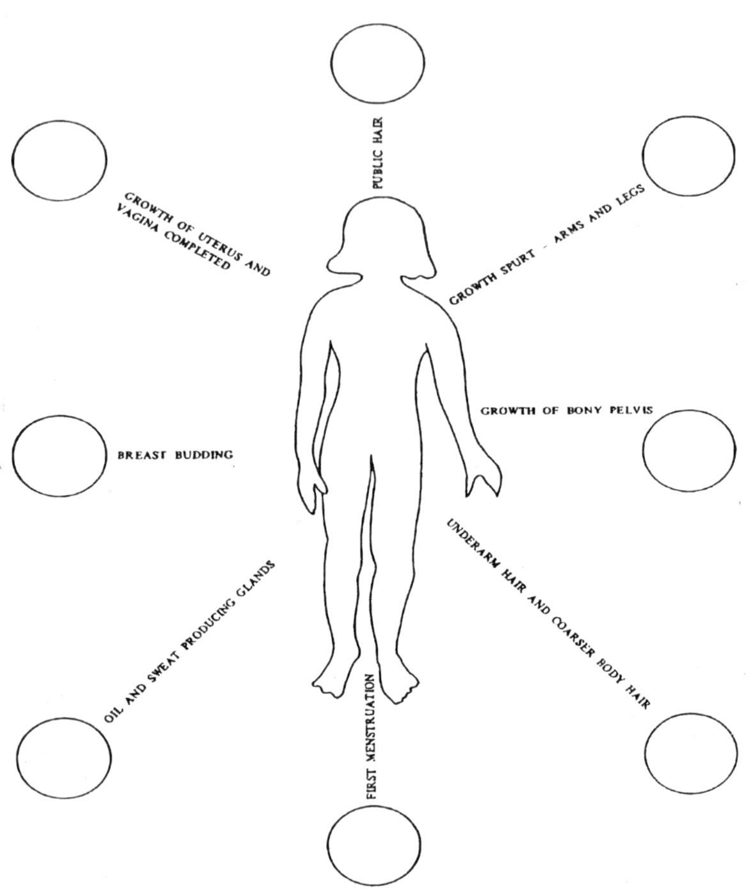

The Body Clock

Many changes happen during puberty. Place a number from 1 to 8 in each circle to show the order ylou think these changes take place.

Worksheet 1.4.2 The Male Body Clock

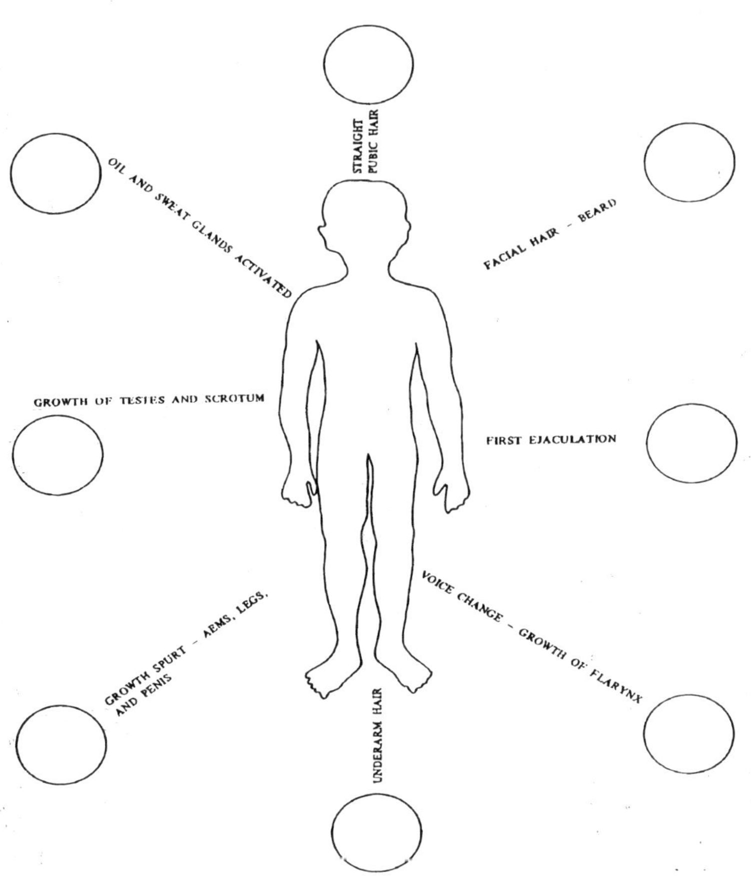

The Body Clock

Many changes happen during puberty. Place a number from 1 to 8 in each circle to show the order ylou think these changes take place.

1.5 LOOKING AT MYSELF AS I SEE MY BODY

Objectives :

(1) To identify the adolescents' feelings abut the various parts or aspects of their bodies.

(2) To help the students increase their self—awareness and self-esteem by assessing house parts of their body which they are satisfied with, and those parts which they would like to improve.

Time Required: 40 minutes

Material: Information Sheet Activities

PROCEDURE

1. Lecture on self-esteem and self-concept of adolescents based on the information sheet.

2. Distribute copies of "Looking at Myself" chart.

3. Give the students 10 to 15 minute to fill out the chart.

4. Break the class into groups of about four or five. Have each student in the group spend about two minutes sharing at least three things he/she likes about him/herself (and why), and at least one thing he/she is proud of doing. Before they begin, set up ground rules with the class.

5. Every two minutes or so, remind the groups to move on to the next student to make sure that everyone gets a chance to share his/her views.

6. When everyone has spoken, open the discussion in the large group by asking questions similar to the following:

   — What did it feel like to share your personal views?

   — Do you find it hard to say positive things about yourself in a group?

   — Were you surprised by anything that was said?

   — How do we learn to like ourselves? How important is it to like ourselves?

7. Have the students work on their own charts to bring home the following points:

   a. We are all made up of many parts.

   b. Some parts we like and some we don't.

c. We can either learn to accept the parts we don't like or change them—we have a choice.

d. By remembering the parts we like we feel more sure of ourselves and more able to accomplish things.

e. By focusing on the concept of liking ourselves we feel good when we are with other people and we feel better about everything we do.

8. The earlier activity serves as an opportunity for the students to think about how people feel about different parts of their bodies. Explain that people are of different sizes and shapes and often a person may feel very good about his/her physical appearance. For the lecture on self-esteem and self-concept, use Information Sheet p.73.

9. The suggested activity 1.5.2 can be used to determine the students' ideas on body image and how they view their physical appearance. You may also ask them about why they have negative attitudes to certain parts of the body. Ask, for example; "How many of you believe that most people like their feet and (have them note the responses of their classmates).

10. After you have questioned the class about various body parts, duplicate and distribute worksheet 1.5.2. Tell the students that they are about to have an opportunity to think about how they see their own bodies and to ask themselves how they feel about each of the parts listed on the worksheet. Point out that their worksheets will not have their names, so they can feel free to express their real feelings.

11. When the students have finished their worksheets, ask the following questions:

    a) What do you think it means to be attractive?

    b) Do you think that someone who like his/her body would feel better about himself/herself than someone who doesn't?

    c) Are your responses heavily concentrated under a specific column?

d) What do you think a person could do to change the way he/she feels about his/her body?

12. As an optional part of this activity, collect the worksheets from students and tally the responses for the body parts listed. The totals are reported back to the students. (NOTE: The tallies can be a specific or a general tally. In a specific tally, numerical tallies of specific responses are made. For instance, it can be reported that 20 students said they are happy about their height; eight said they felt very pleased, and two said they had never thought about it. In a general tally, the worksheets are reviewed in a general way to obtain the trend of responses. For example, it can be reported that "Most of the students were happy about their height; some said they felt very pleased, and a few said they hadn't thought about it".

13. Sharing responses with classmates helps create a general awareness among students of the similarities and differences in their feelings about their bodies. it is also helpful to share the fact that these feelings are normal and that certain parts of the male, female body are better liked than the others.

14. To summarize this activity, explain that self-knowledge and self-esteem are crucial to our manner of expressing ourselves to others. Point out the possibility of changing certain aspects of our physical appearance, as for example, by dieting or cutting our hair. However these options are limited. Tell the students that people derive a great deal of happiness from being able to recognize the possibilities for change and accepting their uniqueness and the special persons that they are.

INFORMATION SHEET

Self-Esteem

Self-esteem is closely identified with self-respect. It includes a proper regard for oneself as a human being and an accurate sense of one's personal place within the larger society of family, friends, associates, and others. In the extreme, self-esteem can degenerate into conceit, while a lack of it can result in a sense of unworthiness. The key is balance. Too much focus on self causes the inflation of conceit blocking the experience of cooperative relationships. On the other hand, A deficient sense of self, makes one unable to interact freely and responsibly with others at home, in school, in work and in society.

Parents and teachers have the greatest influence on children's self-esteem. Children's experience of being loved and lovable during the early years form their self-concept- and self-esteem. Harris Clemes and Reynold Bean have defined the following four conditions that must be fulfilled in order for a high sense of self-esteem to be developed and maintained.

> *Connectiveness*, that results when a child gains satisfaction from associations that are significant to the child and the importance of these associations has been affirmed by others.
>
> *Uniqueness*, that occurs when a child can acknowledge and respect the qualities or attributes that make him/her special and different, and receives respect and approval from others for these qualities.
>
> *Power*, that comes about through having the resources, opportunity, and capability to influence the circumstances of his/her own life in important ways.
>
> *Models*, that reflect a child's ability to refer to adequate human, philosophical, and operational examples that serve to help him/her establish meaningful values, goals, ideals and personal standards.*

It is important to a student's self-esteem that the school provide experiences that satisfy these four conditions every day, that learning itself becomes self—enhancing. Most important are successful relationships with peers and teachers and the satisfaction of academic achievement. Second to these are learning experiences specifically designed to build self-esteem while providing cognitive learning.

The importance of positive self-regard should not be minimized or given only token acknowledgment. Self-esteem is the foundation upon which personal and social development is based. Indeed, to a considerable degree, personal success can be measured in terms of how well one has succeeded in constructing an accurate model of himself/herself in relation to others.

While a person's sense of self is ever changing, reflecting the flux of events both internal and external, students at the upper elementary level are at a crucial period of development: a period of life when the self-images of early childhood broaden out into the more encompassing visions of adolescence. The child's personal experience of the world expands, taking in ever-widening spheres of interest and accomplishment. Self-understanding in relation to others, the development of a positive and accurate sense of self, can have immense significance. It affects one's sense of personal success within the family, at school, and elsewhere.

Self Concept

Self-concept can be defined as a person's perception of himself. This incudes his perception of his abilities, character, attitudes, traits, appearance, aims and deeds. Other terms such as self-image, self-evaluation, self-esteem are used in lieu of self-concept.

Self-concept is described as the directing force in human behaviour because a person acts consistent to his/her self-concept. In other words, what a person thinks or how he behaves is determined largely by the concept he holds about himself. A person who is confident and has high regard for himself behaves differently from another person, who feels incompetent, inferior and insecure. Similarly, a person who feels competent in one situation behaves differently in another situation where he feels incompetent in one situation behaves differently in another situation where he feels incompetent and insecure. His behaviour can further reinforce his perception of himself. A person who perceives himself as a poor reader makes so many mistakes when asked to read. Therefore his self-image as a poor reader is reinforced. Often we are afraid to try because we feel we are not good enough.

A person perceives, interprets,accepts, rejects or resists what he encounters in accordance to his self-image. His behaviour may appear irrational to observers but to the person, they are consistent to the stimuli as perceived by him. To the onlooker, a headmaster's authoritarian behaviour in school is contradictory to his submissive behaviour at home. But to the headmaster his behaviour is consistent to his perception of his roles-just as he expects the teacher and students under his supervision or his domain to adhere to his rules and regulations he expects similar behaviour from himself at home where it is his wife's domain.

Our self-concept is formed through interaction with people. From the way others react towards us and the appraisals they make of our efforts, we form concepts of who we are and what we are capable of achieving. Consequently, the reactions of people, especially of those who are significant to us, will influence the formation of our self-concept.

SUGGESTED ACTIVITY 1.5.1

In using the "Looking at Myself" chart, tell the students that they have to list at least 8 things they like about themselves (Junior high students find it much easier to list things they don't like). The chart also separates physical attributes from personality. It is especially difficult for young adolescents to say positive things about their body. Their bodies are still rapidly changing and their self-concepts are not yet firmly established. As a lead into more in depth discussions in later sessions, start the discussion on the changes that occur during puberty.

Looking At Myself

What I like about Myself (at least 8 things):

Physical Characteristics	*Personality Characteristics*

What I don't Like About Myself:

Physical Characteristics	*Personality Characteristics*

Things I would like to change or Improve about myself:	How I might Do this:

Things I am Proud of doing:

SUGGESTED ACTIVITY 1.5.2

Directions: Here is a list of parts of the body and common reactions to these parts. Think about your body, and how you feel about each of these parts. Place a check mark in the column which best describes how you feel.

Worksheet 1.4.2

Part of Body	Very Ok	Sort of Ok	Definitely Not ok	Never Thought About it
1. Face				
2. Hair				
3. Eyes				
4. Ears				
5. Nose				
6.Teeth				
7. Voice				
8. Arms				
9. Hands				
10. Feet				
11. Waist/stomach				
12. Hips/buttocks				
13. Legs/thighs				
14. Body hair				
15. Height				
16. Weight				

1.6 CONCEPTION

Objectives :

To familiarize students with basic knowledge about the physiological processes of human conception

Time Required : 60 Minutes

Material : Information Sheets and Worksheets

Worksheet 1.6.1 Conception

Worksheet 1.6.2 Fertilization

Worksheet 1.6.3 Conception

PROCEDURE

1. Present an introductory lecture on conception, refer to the Information Sheet.

2. Using worksheets 1.6.1 to 1.6.3 to illustrate the point, explain that the ability to reproduce is basic to the perpetuation and continuation of all forms of life. These illustrations can be duplicated and distributed to the students, or shown on an opaque projector. Explain that the union of male and female cells causes new life to begin.

3. Tell students that in mammals, such as human beings, fertilization occurs during the process of sexual intercourse. (Mention some recent scientific advances that allow fertilization in ways not previously thought possible, such as artificial insemination and the test-tube baby.) Emphasize that at the moment of conception, the individual is already unique, and facial features, hair colour, and other features are formed.

4. In teaching concepts about conception, be sure to check the policies and guidelines concerning family life and sex education specific to your district and/or school. When possible, enlist the parents involvement to ensure the continuation of the learning process at home with the student. Remember that parents are the primary sex educators of children and that curriculum materials presented

in the classroom are intended to supplement and further the aims of parents in educating their children. When you believe students have a good basic understanding of the concepts and processes involved in concepts, you can follow up with the Suggested Activity.

INFORMATION SHEET

Teaching about conception

Conception, since it involves intercourse, is a sensitive topic. Parents can help set guidelines for explaining intercourse. They may want questions about intercourse referred to them-therefore seek their participation or assistance. Check the guidelines of your school district before presenting any material on this topic. Be aware of state education codes that require parental preview of all materials used in the classroom. Encourage students to discuss this lesson with their parents. You might suggest that the students show the worksheets and illustrations to their parents.

1. Conception

A. The ability to reproduce is necessary for the continuation of the human race. New life occurs when male and female sex cells unite at conception.

B. The sex cells are needed to give birth to a new life. These sex cells are given the change to fuse and form a new life during sexual intercourse.

C. In mammals, such as human beings, conception begins with the act of intercourse. During intercourse, sperm from the man's penis is deposited in the women's vagina.

D. The semen of the male which contains millions of sperms is deposited in the vagina of the female. The sperms, once deposited in the vagina, make their way at a very rapid rate to the uterus and the fallopian tubes (see worksheet 1.6.1)

E. As sperms reach the fallopian tubes where an ovum is likely to be found, fertilization takes place.

F. Fertilization occurs in five processes. The first process is the penetration which occurs when the outer layer of the sperm unites with the membrane surrounding the ovum. In the second process, a union takes place where the contents of the sperm head have access to the ovum. In the third process, the sperm as a whole enters the ovum. During the fourth process called activation, the ovum develops a reaction which prevents other sperms from gaining entry to it. The last process involves the fusion of nuclear materials from the two sex cells after which cell division takes place.

G. After fertilization, the fertilized ovum which has become a zygote travels from the fallopian tube to the uterus.

H. As the fertilized ovum or zygote travels, a series of events and changes begins to take place. First, the zygote undergoes cell division. It divides into two cells, then four, then eight, then sixteen and so on. Three to five days after fertilization, the zygote reaches the uterus (see worksheets 1.6.4).

I. In the uterus, the cell implants itself. The cell divides itself into ectoderm or outer skin which will cover the outer surface of the body and the endoderm or inner skin which will line the inner surface.

J. Cells in the position of the ectoderm nearest the inner skin further multiply to form the skin and the nervous system. The rest of the outer skin become the amnion, the membrane which envelops the embryo. Then the mesoderm is developed to form the connective tissues, bones, muscles, blood vessels.

K. Six to seven days after fertilization, implantation occurs. The zygote which has become the blastocyst penetrates and sinks into the uterine lining or endometrium.

L. Sometimes, the blastocyst cannot travel from the fallopian tube to the uterus. Instead, it implants itself in the walls of the fallopian tube. In such rare cases, fertilization and implantation take place in the ovary. Whether the pregnancy is tubal or ovarian, the general term used is ectopic pregnancy.

M. At the moment of conception the genes and chromosomes from the mother and father unite to form a unique individual with particular traits and characteristics.

N. Occasionally two ova are released at the same time. If this happens, it is possible for both to be fertilized and fraternal twins to be conceived. Identical twins are a result of the division of one fertilized ovum into two completely separate cells that then continue to develop into two babies. Siamese twins are extremely rare. These are identical twins that started to separate but some part of the body remained joined. Surgeons may try to separate the two infants after birth. Sometimes both survive, sometimes one, sometimes neither.

SUGGESTED ACTIVITY

Below are 10 statements describing the various stages of fertilization. Number the stages represented by statements chronologically from 1 to 10.

—(A) In the uterus, the cell implants itself.

—(B) Six to seven days after fertilization, implantation occurs. The zygote which has become the blastocyst penetrates and sinks into the uterine lining or endometrium.

—(C) During sexual intercourse, the semen of the male which contains millions of sperms is deposited in the vagina.

—(D) The fertilized ovum which has become a zygote travels from the fallopian tube to the uterus.

—(E) The sperms, once deposited in the vagina, make their way to the uterus and the fallopian tube where an ovum is likely to be found.

—(F) When the sperm reaches an ovum fertilization occurs in five processes.

—(G) The cell divides itself into an ectoderm and an endoderm.

—(H) As the zygote travels after fertilization it undergoes cell division into two, then four, then eight, then 16 and son on.

—(I) Then the mesoderm is developed to form the connective tissues, bones, muscles, blood and blood vessels.

—(J) Sometimes, the blastocyst implants itself in the walls of the fallopian tube resulting in ectopic pregnancy.

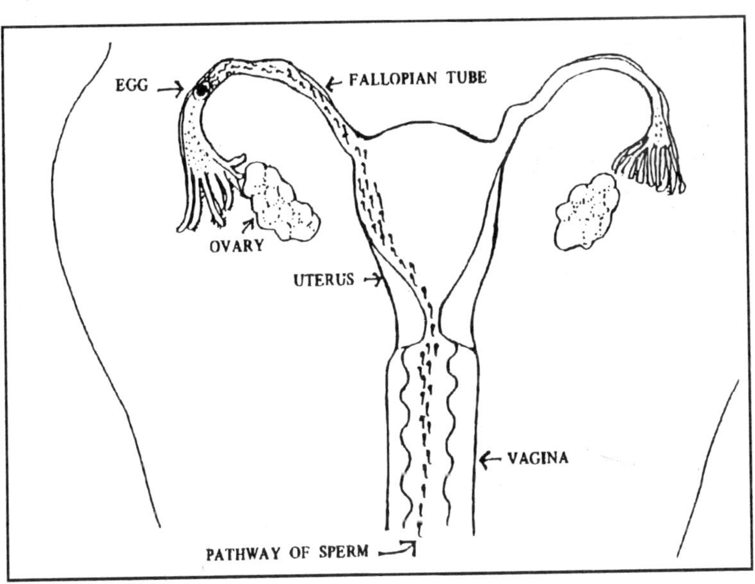

Worsheet 1.6.1 Pathway of Sperm

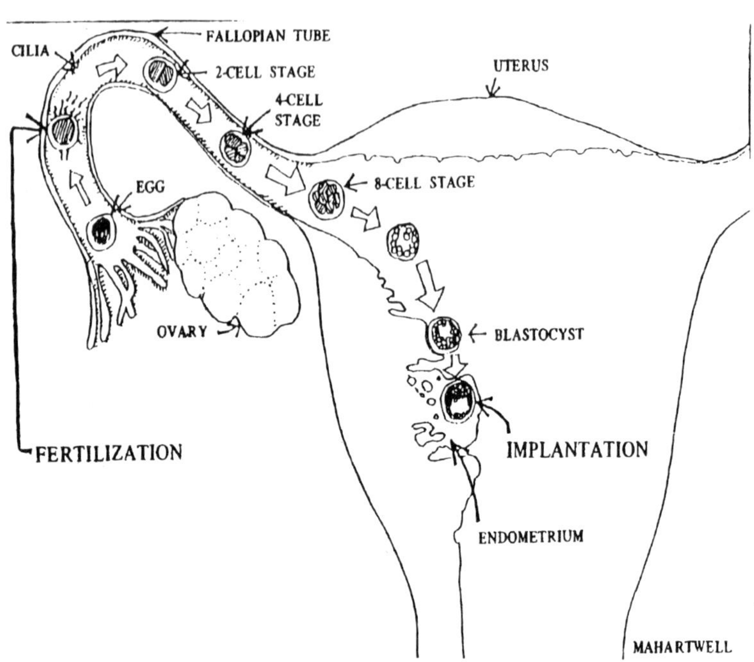

Worsheet 1.6.2 Pathway of Fertilized Egg

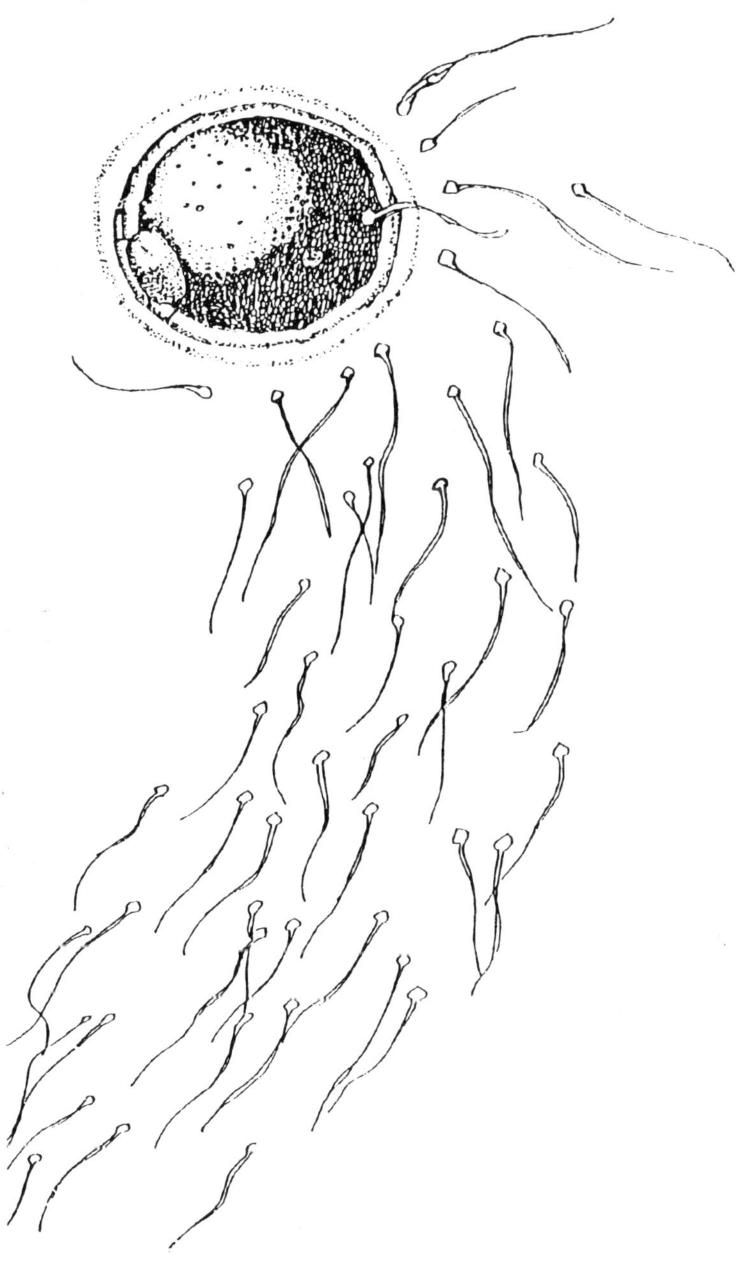

Worsheet 1.6.3 Fertilization

Worsheet 1.6.4 Cell Division During Fertilization

The Sperm contains 23 chromosomes and so does the ovum (all other cells in the human body contain 2 x 23 = 46 chromosomes). One of the 23 chromosomes in both the ovum and in the sperm is a sex-chromosome. When the sperm and the ovum fuse they create an entirely new cell with 46.

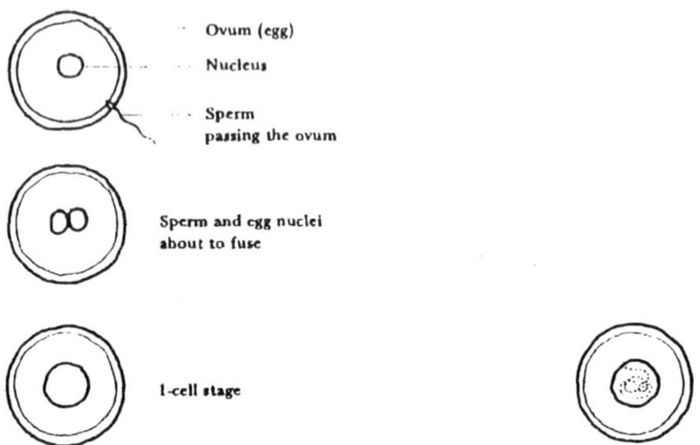

Now this cell begins to divide; first into two cells then into four, then eight and so on.

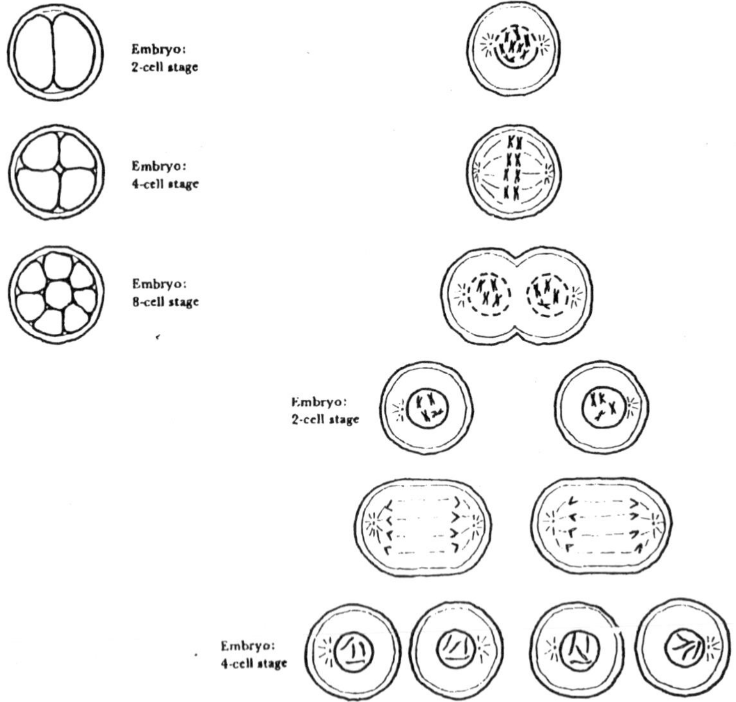

1.7 PREGNANCY AND ESSENTIAL NEEDS

Objectives :

(1) To provide the students with basic knowledge concerning the physiological processes in pregnancy.

(2) To make students aware of the signs and symptoms of pregnancy.

(3) To make them understand the importance of antenatal care and essential needs during pregnancy.

Time Required : 60 minutes

Materials : Information Sheets and Worksheets

Worksheet 1.7.1	Embryo after 6 weeks and after 10 weeks of pregnancy
Worksheet 1.7.2	Embryo after 14 weeks of pregnancy (ac-tual size)
Worksheet 1.7.3	Full term foetus (actual size)
Worksheet 1.7.4	24 weeks of pregnancy (actual size)

PROCEDURE

1. This lesson has two parts. The first part deals with the physiological processes involved in pregnancy, while the second part focuses on signs and symptoms of pregnancy and prenatal care.

2. Present two lectures on both aspects using the Information Sheets. For the lecture on prenatal development, use Worksheets 1.7.1 to 1.7.4

3. To introduce pregnancy, focus on the changes occurring to the foetus. Discuss with the students the effect of the mother's health and nutrition on the developing foetus. Also explain that both parents experience emotional changes during pregnancy, although only the mother experiences the direct physical changes. Students may also be interested to learn about multiple births, the causes of birth defects, and how the foetus breathes, receives nour-

ishment, and excretes while in *utero.*

4. After the lecture, have students do activities 1.7.1 to 1.7.3.

INFORMATION SHEET

1. Teaching About Pregnancy

A. Adolescents are fascinated by pregnancy and birth, especially the unusual: twins, birth defects, Siamese twins. They'll also want to understand how the foetus can live inside the sack of water, how it eats, breathes, and urinates.

B. One of the most important ideas to get across is that anyone who is sexually active should be especially careful of their health and the substances he takes into his body. Young people need to be aware that drug and alcohol use by both parents, especially by the mother during the pregnancy may possibly harm the baby.

C. Films and pictures on foetal development will greatly enhance this presentation. Assign groups of students to research on the development of the foetus at each month of growth and to construct a chart on this development.

D. Encourage students to share the information from class with their parents. The worksheets and illustrations may be taken home to give parents and children an opportunity to discuss pregnancy together.

II. PREGNANCY

A. The fertilized ovum, now called the embryo, embeds itself in the lining of the uterus where it will grow and develop until it is born.

   1. The human foetus lives inside the mother for nine months. This is called the gestation period.

   2. About one week after conception, the cells begin to specialize. Some will form skin, others nerve, bone, blood or glands.

   3. Some cells develop into the placenta which is the organ that supplies the foetus with oxygen and

nutrition. It also carries off the foetal waste products.

4. The placenta is attached to the foetus by the umbilical cord.

B. It is about this time that the mother may miss a period and suspect that she is pregnant.

1. It is important that she takes care of herself even before she suspects she is pregnant, since, the first two weeks are so vitally important to the health of the embryo.

2. It is also important for the women to see a doctor or nurse-midwife early and to continue to have regular visit to check on the foetus development and the mother's health.

3. The mother should choose her food carefully to get plenty of vitamins, minerals and protein.

a. No drugs, even aspirin, should be taken during pregnancy unless prescribed by a physician.

b. Alcohol can be very dangerous to the foetus if not taken in moderation. It can cause damage to its pancreas, liver and brain.

c. Mothers who smoke are more likely to have babies who are of low weight at birth, and consequently more susceptible to illness and disease.

d. Harmful or unhealthy substances taken into the mother's body will reach the foetus and cause much harm to it.

C. For the next few weeks the foetus continues to develop until, by the end of the second month-though less than one inch long—its limbs, hands, and feet are fully formed. The foetus moves and reacts to stimulus. Scientists have demonstrated, by touching the foetus in utero and observing reflexive movement, that the foetus has developed its sense of feeling. At this point, the foetus looks just like a very little baby.

D. The foetus lives in the amniotic sac. This sac is filled with fluid which acts as a cushion to protect the foetus.

1. The amniotic fluid may be swallowed by the foetus and then excreted as urine into the fluid. The fluid is continually cleaned and replenished.

2. The foetal oxygen supply comes through the umbilical cord from the placenta. Because it gets its oxygen in this manner, the foetus does not use its lungs to breathe and therefore can live in the amniotic fluid.

3. The foetus receives its food through the umbilical cord also. Nutrients enter through the cord to nourish the foetus and promote growth.

4. Waste products, such as carbon dioxide and food wastes, pass out of the foetal body through the umbilical cord, eventually into the mother's veins, and are then passed out of her body.

E. Sometimes the foetus doesn't develop correctly and the body expels it long before the gestation period is over. When this happens, it's called a miscarriage. The foetus is too immature to survive and the pregnancy is ended.

F. During the last three months of pregnancy, the foetus has a well developed brain and sensory awareness. While inside the mother, the foetus sees shadows through its mother's abdominal wall and is aware of light and dark. The foetus is able to hear the internal sounds from the mother and even loud noises outside the mother's body.

G. Although the gestation period usually lasts about 280 days, some babies are born sooner. Babies born before they have completed the gestation period are called premature and need special care in the hospital until they are mature enough to go home.

H. As the gestation period ends, the completely developed foetus (usually turned to a head-down position) waits for birth.

PREGNANCY

Conception and Essential Needs During Pregnancy

Conception is the beginning of a new life resulting from the meeting of sperm and an ovum. On conception, women experience the common signs and symptoms of pregnancy which may vary and occur earlier or later in different women.

Signs and Symptoms at various Stages of pregnancy

Early stage:	Amenorrhoea =	menstruation stops
	Nausea =	a feeling of wanting to throw up, commonly experienced on rising in the morning or even in the evening.
Mid-Term Stage	Frequent micturition= urinating frequently Enlargement of the breasts with darkening of the nipples. Enlargement of the abdomen and uterus is palpable= (can feel the uterus) Quickening= foetal movements felt Breast changes are more pronounced and secretion of milk (build up of colostrum) is present.	
Late Stage :	Uterus has very much increased in size and foetal parts and movements felt Foetus becomes viable, that is, capable of an independant existence	

Importance of Prenatal Care

The average duration of human pregnancy is 280 days or 40 weeks or 9 calendar months and a week. Pregnancy is a natural phenomenon and majority of expectant mothers would experience good health and promote the healthy growth of the foetus if she would have adequate prenatal care provided at the various clinics, urban or rural, government or private. Pre-natal care is an important part of the total care of pregnant women and the services provide:-

- Guidance and health supervision
- Delivery service
- Learning the art of child care
- Motivating for family spacing
- Encouraging family life development

ESSENTIAL NEEDS DURING PREGNANCY

a. Regular attendance at Antenatal Clinic

It is important that mothers attend the prenatal clinic services on a regular basis so as to receive quality care and maintain optimum health for herself and her unborn baby. The normal pregnant mother should visit the clinic at least about eight times during her current pregnancy so as to have continuous health care and medical supervision.

The first clinic attendance should be scheduled after about 12 weeks, followed by 6 weeks—interval up to 30th week, and fortnightly visits until 40th week. Frequency of clinic visits by high risk mothers depends on the condition of each individual mother and the decision of her physician.

b. Balance diet

An adequate well-balance diet is essential for health. In pregnancy it is of particular importance to maintain the health of the mother in order to ensure food for the growing baby. Intake of nutritious food, the right amount of each kind of food during pregnancy will also help to promote a successful lactation which is ideal for the baby. It has now been established that breast-feeding helps to lay the foundation of sound emotional health of the child.

The daily diet should consist of balanced meals containing the following: a) Body-building food such as fish, meat, poultry, eggs, milk and pulses such as green peas, lentils, red beans, peanuts, soya-beans, etc; b) Energy giving food such such as rice, yam, potatoes, bread and cereals; c) Some fats, oil, butter or margarine; (d) Body protecting food such as green leafy vegetables, beans, tomatoes, carrots, cabbage and a variety of local fruits such as papaya, mangoes, guavas, star fruit.

Since a woman needs special dietary care during pregnancy the family members should cut expenses on less essential things to ensure adequate supply of food. A home garden could be cultivated by the family.

c. Exercise

Exercise during pregnancy helps to stimulate circulation, maintain good posture, strengthen the muscle and increase the ability to relax. Most women get a certain amount of exercise while doing housework. The kind and amount of exercise a mother needs depends on the type of work she does.

Manual women workers who do heavy work should actually lighten their load of work as pregnancy advances.

Housewives may need moderate exercise particularly in the open air walking or gardening is beneficial.

Sedentary women who have very little exercise should do specific exercise daily.

d. Rest, relaxation and sleep

Extra rest is necessary and relaxation needs practice. Relaxation is a way of conditioning the muscles, to loosen up and help to release tension. The mother should take every opportunity to rest and learn to relax. She could do this by lying on a mat or a firm mattress, close her eyes tightly then relax followed in like manner by the neck, trunk and limbs. Once the mother has learnt the art of relaxing completely, she will fall asleep afterwards. The expectant mother should aim at eight hours of sleep at night and at least an hour of rest during the day.

e. Emotional support

Certain emotional changes may occur in pregnancy which need to be understood by the expectant mother and her family. The individual personality will influence to a marked degree the exact pattern of emotional change in pregnancy. The general excitable temperament may be increased during pregnancy, hence the women of slow equable temperament may become quite vivacious. Even the placid women may become irritable, uneasy and anxious. The husband should understand the moods and give her the support and assurance that this is a natural happening. When there are social and economic pressures especially if the pregnancy was not planned, the mother may experience feelings of rejection and depression. Loving kindness by the family may help to overcome this stressful period. Each family member could contribute in one way or another towards the well being of the mother and the new member. Planning and sharing the experience will draw the family close together. The midwife and the physician may also play a supportive role to maintain the emotional health of the expectant mother.

DEFINITIONS AND TERMINOLOGY

Prenatal	-	Care of the woman during pregnancy, before giving birth
Birth	-	Process by which a baby is moved from the uterus to the outside world
Conception	-	Fertilization of an egg cell by a sperm cell
Duration of pregnancy	-	From the first day of the mother's last menstrual period of delivery
First trimester	-	From 1st day of last menstrual period up to 12th completed weeks
Second trimester	-	13th to 25th completed week
Third trimester	-	26th weeks to delivery
Gestational Age	-	Duration of gestation as measured from the first day of last menstruation expressed in completed days or weeks.
Primigravida	-	A woman who is pregnant for the first time
Gravida	-	A women who has had several pregnancies
Primipara	-	A women who has borne one child
Parity	-	Number of pregnancies reaching viability
Prenatal	-	Before birth
Natal	-	Pertaining to birth
Post natal	-	After birth
Post natal care	-	Care of the mother covering about six weeks after delivery to recuperate her to normal health.

Stages of Development of the Unborn Child

Embryo	-	From the first to 7 completed weeks of

		gestation
Foetus	-	From 8 weeks to birth
Newborn	-	Foetus after the umbilical cord is ligated up to 27 completed days
pregnancy	-	The condition of a women from conception to delivery

SUGGESTED ACTIVITY 1.7.1

Placed check(✓) mark before the correct answer.

1. The human foetus normally lives inside the mother for:

______________ a) six months
______________ b) ten months
______________ c) nine months

2. The organ which supplies the foetus with oxygen and nutrition is the:

______________ a) umbilical cord
______________ b) placenta
______________ c) amniotic sac

3. The foetus lives in this place which is filed with fluid and which acts as a cushion to protect it:

______________ a) amniotic sac
______________ b) placenta
______________ c) uterus

4. The placenta is attached to the foetus by the:

______________ a) fallopian tube
______________ b) umbilical cord
______________ c) cells

5. The limbs, hands and feet of the foetus become fully developed by:

______________ a) two weeks
______________ b) the end of the second month
______________ c) one month

6. Waste products such as carbon dioxide and food wastes pass out of the foetal body into the mother's veins and out her body through the:

______________ a) rectum
______________ b) intestines

_______________ c) umbilical cord

7. When the foetus has not developed correctly and the mother's body expels it long before the gestation period is over, this is called:

_______________ a) abortion
_______________ b) labour
_______________ c) miscarriage

8. During the last three months of pregnancy, the foetus:-

_______________ a) is just developing its limbs, legs and feet
_______________ b) has turned to a head-down position
_______________ c) could see shadows and hear internal sounds from the mother

9. The gestation period lasts for:

_______________ a) 280 days
_______________ b) 450 days
_______________ c) 200 days

10. During pregnancy, the following should not be taken by the mother:

_______________ a) soft drinks
_______________ b) alcohol and drugs like aspirin
_______________ c) sugar

SUGGESTED ACTIVITY 1.7.2

Conception, Development and Birth

Direction: Select the term from Column B that is most appropriate to the phrase in Column A by writing the letter of your answer on the space provided.

Column A	Column B
1. The event that occurs when a sperm penetrates and fuses with an egg.	a) Foetus
2. An unborn child developing in the uterus from the first to the 7th week of life.	b) Newborn
3. The rope-like structure through which food and energy are carried from the mother to the unborn child.	c) Embryo

4. The network of blood vessels and tissues by which the unborn child is attached to the uterus. d) Conception

5. The muscular contractions that expel a baby from the uterus. e) pregnancy

6. The baby after the umbilical cord is ligated to 27 days of life. f) Placenta

7. The beginning of a new life resulting from the fusing of a sperm and ovum. g) Fertilization

SUGGESTED ACTIVITY 1.7.3

Film: "A Child is Born"

Direction: Watch the film carefully to obtain the information requested below. At the end of the film write down the information you obtained from the film.

Signs and symptoms of pregnancy:

a.
b.
c.
d.

Prenatal care measures:

a.
b.
c
d.

The mother's needs during pregnancy:

a.
b.
c.
d.

Admission and preparation measures for delivery:

a.
b.
c.
d.

Signs of commencement and progress of labour:

a.

b.

c.

d.

Birth process and care of the newborn:

a.

b.

c.

d.

Ideal conditions of a mother before pregnancy:

a.

b.

c.

d.

What are the right conditions for a mother during pregnancy?

a.

b.

c.

d.

Question for discussion:

1. What are the signs and symptoms of pregnancy?
2. Why is it important to have prenatal care?
3. What are the essential needs during pregnancy?
    a. Mother's needs
    b. Foetus needs
4. What is a balanced diet?
5. What are suitable exercises for expectant mothers?
6. What is the value of rest, relaxation and sleep?

Worksheet 1.7.1 Embryo After 6 Weeks and After 10 Weeks

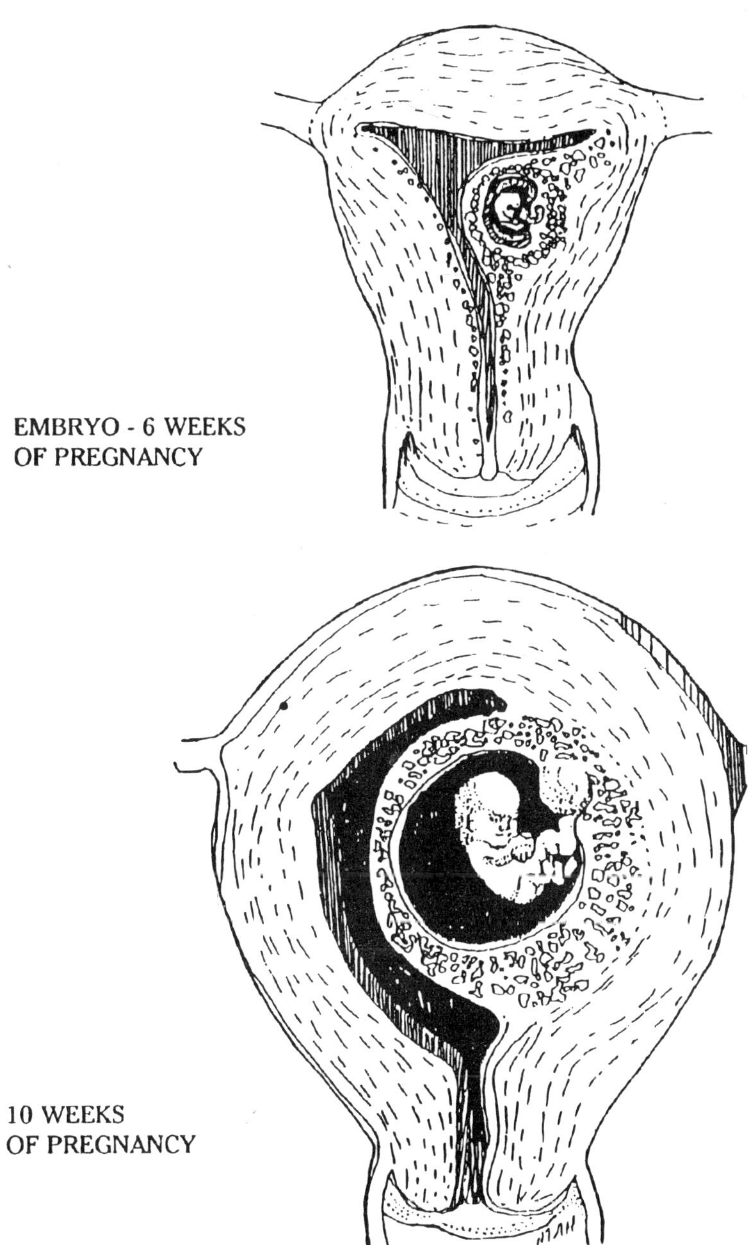

Worksheet 1.7.2 Embryo After 14 Weeks of Pregnancy

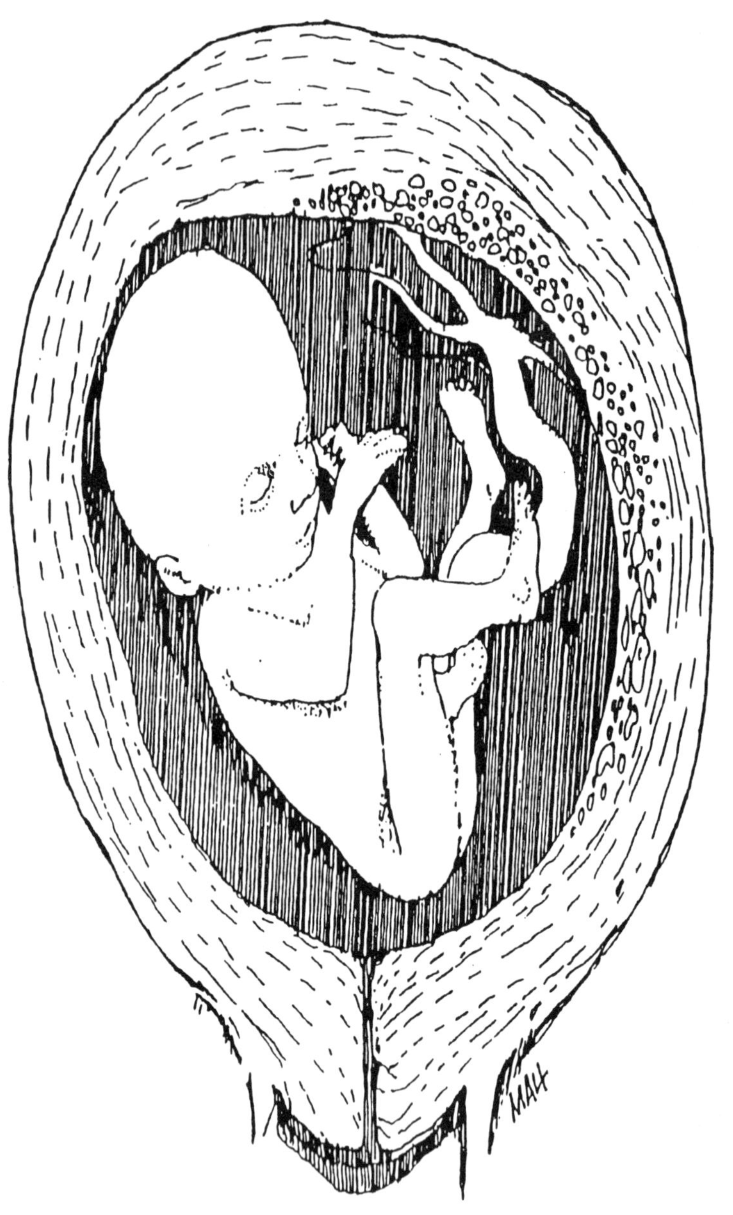

Worksheet 1.7.3 Full Term Foetus (I)

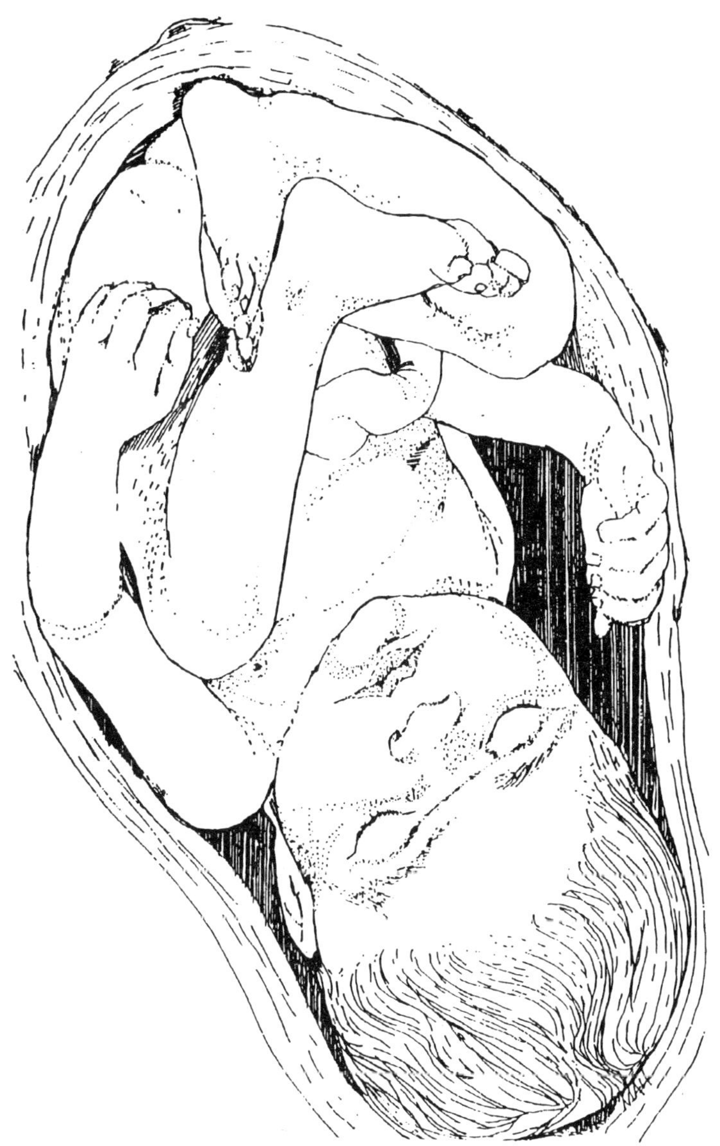

Worksheet 1.7.3 Full Term Foetus (ii)

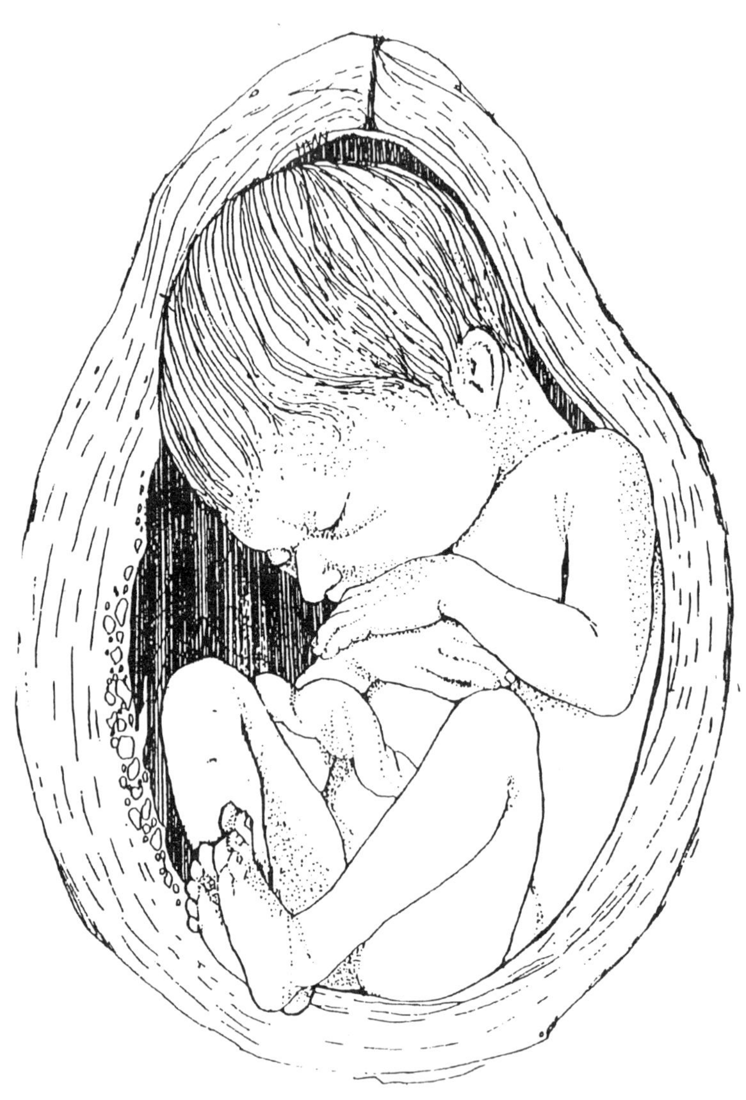

MODULE 2

SOCIAL ASPECTS

2

SOCIAL ASPECTS

This is the second of a series of four modules that comprises a package entitled Adolescence Education.

This Module on social aspects deals with the sociological and cultural aspects of human sexuality. It covers such topics as sexual behaviour, sexuality in childhood and adolescence, love, dating and relationship, adolescent pregnancy and moral code of ethics. This module consists of the following lessons and their corresponding objectives.

Topics	Objectives
Lesson 2.1 Adolescent Sexuality/ Sexual Behaviour	(1) To develop an understanding and apprecia tion of sex drive as a natural aspect of growing up. (2) To describe some manifestations of the sex drive in the adolescent. (3) To explain the importance of controlling and guiding the sex drive. (4) To explain the various factors that influence the development of sexual attitudes and behaviour. (5) To realize the importance of wholesome sexual attitudes and behaviour. (6) To accept the need to control and guide one's sex drive for it to become a positive force in a person's life.

	(7) To evaluate issues related to the sex drive.
Lesson 2.2 Sexuality in Childhood and Adolescence	(1) To discuss the development of sexuality from childhood to adolescence. (2) To differentiate between pregenital and genital sexuality. (3) To identify specific behaviours that adolescents exhibit during social and emotional maturation or development. (4) To discuss the various problems of adolescents and to offer solutions to these problems,
lesson 2.3 Love	(1) To understand the concept of love and the different types of love. (2) To differentiate between mature and im mature love. (3) To list ways of showing love to one´s parents, friends, girlfriend/boyfriend.
Lesson 2.4 Dating and Relationship	(1) To understand the various dating customs throughout the world. (2) To define what dating is and identify the objectives of dating. (3) To Study various attitudes towards dating. (4) To identify what is an ideal dating partner. (5) To solve problems related to dating.
Lesson 2.5 Adolescent Pregnancy	(1) To discuss the growing number of adolescent pregnancies and the consequences of adolescent pregnancy and parenting both in the pre-marital and marital situations. (2) To explore individual feelings and attitudes about adolescent pregnancy and sexual behaviour.
Lesson 2.6 Morale Code of Ethics-Their Roles and Functions	(1) To understand what is meant by code of ethics or morality. (2) To be aware of the complexities and difficulties involved in deciding what is morally right or wrong. (3) To be aware of the existence of various theories on moral behaviour. (4) To understand the concept of morality in relation to the family, peers, religion, culture, education and political system, with emphasis on the confusion and conflicts between the older and younger generations.

Each lesson is provided with a set of objectives and indicates the time required for teaching, the materials to be used and the set of procedures to be followed in carrying our the teaching. Information sheets to help teachers in expanding the subject, reference materials and activities/exercises for students are also provided.

2.1 ADOLESCENT SEXUALITY/ SEXUAL BEHAVIOUR

Objectives :

1. To develop an understanding and appreciation of sex drive as a natural aspect of growing up.
2. To describe some manifestations of the sex drive in the adolescent.
3. To explain the importance of controlling and guiding the sex drive.
4. To explain the various factors that influence the development of sexual attitudes and behaviour.
5. To realize the importance of wholesome sexual attitudes and behaviour.
6. To accept the need to control and guide one's sex drive for it to become a positive force in a person's life.
7. To evaluate issues related to sex drive.

Time Required : 4-6 class periods

Materials . Information sheets, chalkboard, marker pens, platform and chairs for panel forum.

PROCEDURE

1. Write the phrase "sex drive" on the chalkboard. Ask the students for their reactions to this term, encouraging them to express their ideas. Write these ideas on the chalkboard.
2. Distribute Activity Sheet 2.1.1. Allow them enough time to read and follow this up with a discussion, using the guide questions suggested after each situation. The dis-

cussions should be based on Information Sheets.

3. After discussing Activity 2.1.1, make a summary using Information Sheet.

4. In the next session, review the previous discussions by stating:

You will recall that one of the characteristics of adolescent boys and girls mentioned in our previous discussion is their attraction towards the opposite sex. Some of you may be going through this experience right now. Teenage boys and girls may sooner or later experience other types of sexual behaviour aside from attraction to the opposite sex. Boys may be having "wet dreams" and erections. Boys and girls may have the desire to fondle their genitals or to masturbate. They may also have a desire for kissing and petting. These desires are all part of the human sex drive or urge that boys and girls go through starting at puberty.

Let us recall the situations. What do you understand by masturbation? Necking? Petting? Wet dreams? Erections? What do you think or feel about these forms of sexual behaviour? Are these normal? Are these "dirty" activities that we should be ashamed of? Why?

5. Encourage the class to give their views and share their problems regarding the human sex drive. If they are shy, tell them to write these on slips of paper without indicating their names. These slips of paper should be collected and read in the class. Have the students react to the views or problems expressed.

6. Many young children realize that their home, religion, society, as well as their peers exert major influences in the development of sexual attitudes. Ask the following questions:

What does your family think about "wet dreams," masturbation, necking, and petting? What is the stand or view of your church (Catholic, Protestant, Islam, etc.) regarding these types of sexual behaviour? What do your friends or peers say about these? What about society in general? Do your home, church, society and peers have the same or con-

flicting views about these sex drives? What do you think of these conflicting views or differences of opinions?

7. It is important that the students be confronted with conflicting views or differences of opinions, and encouraged to discuss them so that they will learn to think and act critically. An example of conflicting views is the double standard on sexual behaviour for men and women. The home or society approves of boys having as many girl friends as they wish, but frowns on girls who behave similarly. Ask the students for their opinion on this inconsistency.

8. Invite a resource person/s to speak on this topic and undertake Suggested Activity 2.1.2.

9. In the third session, inform the students that the discussion topic will focus on the difference between responsible and irresponsible sexual behaviour.

10. Have the students carry out Activities 2.1.3, 2.1.4, 2.1.5.

INFORMATION SHEET

Human Sexuality

The sexual attitudes of the children are formed from earliest childhood, but the sexual urges and forces do not make their appearance until the age of puberty. At this point, many changes occur in the young boy and girl. There is a sudden increase in growth. The secondary sexual characteristics appear, and the shape of the body becomes increasingly that of a woman or man.

In the male, puberty and adolescence begin with the appearance of nocturnal emissions or wet dreams. The penis, testes, and scrotum enlarge, and pubic, auxillary and bodily hair appear. The occurrence of bodily hair in the face, chest, extremities is conditioned by hereditary and racial characteristics, and is therefore, quite variable. The voice of the young boy breaks and attains a deeper tone. The body itself becomes more distinctly muscular.

At about this time, the young man begins to experience a distinct sexual urge or drive. The sexual forces awakened in him make him rather suddenly conscious of the strong sensual pleasure that can be associated with his genitals. There is, in the adolescent, a heightened sexual excitability, which in the male tends to lead to masturbation. This is particularly true of the male because his sexual urges and drives are more distinctly genital. In the adolescent female, the sexual urges are more diffused, and more associated with emotion and daydreams of romantic situations.

The awakened sexual drive produces in the youth, particularly in young men, a certain restlessness of character so that they are often considered by their elders as different and difficult. Their moods are variable. They are impulsive. They find it difficult to concentrate their attention on any thing for any great length of time. Often, even their school performance suffers. The young man is usually more interested in his "barkada", engaging in strenuous physical activities like basketball, swimming, and similar sports. The young women tends to daydream a lot, and her attention is thereby also distracted. In both, there are the first startings towards an independent personality and existence, which tends to show itself as an emotional withdrawal from home and family, and the apparent failure to communicate with and develop an understanding between them and their parents or elders.

This is the critical period of development when parents should exhibit the greatest understanding possible. They should recognize the special features of this awakening sexuality and not misinterpret adolescent behaviour as merely evidences of rebelliousness.

In early adolescence, the young can function sexually at a purely biological plane. Sexual urges can be so strong in the young man that he, in fact, tends to seek sexual gratification at a purely physical level. Sex at this point exists for the sheer pleasure it can provide. It is not in any way associated with emotion or love. It is only later that the young man's psychosexual development will proceed to the point where sex will be increasingly identified with affection.

The young woman, on the other hand, never quite goes through this difficulty. Her sexual drive is less specifically genital, and she tends, from the earliest awakenings of her sexuality, to associate sex with romantic situations. She is also seldom subject to that passing period in the male which has just been described.

As psycho sexual maturity is attained, increasingly, love and sex become more and more clearly identified with one another. Some men who have become so conditioned to sexual expression at the purely physical level, unaware that they are maturing psycho sexually, become ashamed and embarrassed by the fact that when they do fall in love later, that emotion seeks sexual expression. Since their previous experience has always been for the mere pleasure of sex, they feel that they are unworthy if this sexuality is expressed in terms of the object of their love.

Other men never quite reach the degree of sexual maturity where sex is an expression of a deep interpersonal relationship with a woman. These men will continue to seek purely physical or biological sexual gratification throughout their lives in a context outside of the emotion. This means that they have been stunted in the development of their sexuality, and that their personalities are immature.

The Sex Drive

Sexual adjustment is part of the individual's total development into maturity. The maturation of the sex organs, sex characteristics, and sex drives direct the individual along the pathway of development to adult attitudes, and sexual maturity helps to bring out what is best, most generous, and most constructive in the individual's life.

Sex is a basic drive upon which both race reproduction and personal happiness depend. As a drive properly controlled, it becomes a powerful force aiding personal and social adjustment. From a positive point of view, it leads the young away from dependence on their parents and toward independence and the responsibility of loving, supporting, and caring for a family. In this respect, sex is a powerful, constant stimulus toward mature attitudes. If sexuality does not evolve properly, the whole process of growth and development is influenced negatively. Too much repression of sex tends to impair freedom and ease of functioning to the extent that mating and sexual satisfaction are not attained. On the other hand, too much sexual freedom can interfere with normal adjustment in love and mating functions to the degree that sexuality remains on an infantile level, as a desire for play and personal pleasure only. Disturbances in sexual development can lead to personal and social maladjustments.

The sex drive is a natural aspect of life that needs to be both understood and controlled. It should be considered squarely and frankly as a meaningful and respectable part of life. The goal of the sex drive is biological sexual maturity-the capacity to love, mate, reproduce, and care for the young. However, sex has more than reproductive functions; it is an important factor in the partnership between man and woman sharing interests and ideas, mutual acceptance of responsibilities, self-realization and love and as such important for a happy family life.

A person matures sexually years before he can establish a home, and, according to social standard, gives expression to his sexual impulses and desires. He is expected to conform to the conventions within the culture. This means that the sex drive must be controlled if it is to become a positive force in the development of a personality. The requirement for selfcontrol is not unreasonable when one remembers that any great power or drive has to be controlled or its creative force becomes a destructive menace, as illustrated by atomic power. The value of the drive depends upon how skillfully it can be managed.

Self-control motivated from within the individual is more effective than that resulting from outside forces. This implies that the student has the right to know as much as possible about his own sexual adjustment in relation to the demands of society. He needs to know what is expected of him and why. He needs to become familiar with ways and means of exercising control.

1. Sex drive is an impulse related to sex. It is a biological instinct that is necessary for race preservation.

2. The sex drive is manifested in the following:

   a) attraction toward the opposite sex

   b) having "crushes"

c) hero-worship

d) going steady

e) dating

f) etc.

3. Some emotional problems related to the sex drive are:

   a) breaking up of friendships due to a widening of the circle of friends, including members of the opposite sex

   b) Guilt feelings arising from masturbation

   c) teasing

   d) inability to concentrate on anything for any great length of time

   e) daydreaming

   f) etc.

SUGGESTED ACTIVITY 2.1.1

Case studies

Have the students read the following situations. When possible, have copies of these distributed to the students prior to this lesson. Otherwise, the teacher may also write these situations on the chalkboard or on newsprint. Follow this up with a discussion using the guide questions suggested after each situation.

Situation No.1

This letter appeared in the "Dear Fatima" column of a weekly magazine.

"Q. I have a big problem which has kept me from concentrating on my studies. It's about my classmate who's very shy. He doesn't talk to girls, except to those who talk to him first. As days pass, I find my infatuation for him growing. I sometimes think that it is love that I feel. Whenever we are in the classroom, I often look at him, and I am usu-

ally surprised to find him looking at me, too. There are many nights when I can't sleep just thinking about him. I always call him up for a chat. He's very nice, and seems very interested in talking with me over the phone. And yet, when we are in class and I approach him to ask him about something, he is not as nice, and his answers are short. My best friend keeps telling me to stop calling him up because he will think that I am chasing him. She also said that I should leave it up to him to make the first move in communicating with me. But I just can't follow her advice because I am really crazy about him. And since he's too shy to make the first move, I should be the one to do it, don't you think? Please give me your advice".

Guide questions for discussion:

1. What apparently is the problem of the girl who wrote this letter?
2. What feelings are expressed by the writer in her letter?
3. Are her feelings natural? Why do you think so?
4. What term do we give to this intense feeling of attraction toward the opposite sex?
5. Have you experienced this yourself or have you heard of boys and girls who are going or have gone through this experience?
6. If you were in the same situation, what would you have done?

Situation No.2

Haridja and Ayesha have been classmates since the elementary grades. They have always been together, going to and from the school, at lunch and during snack times. Both are enrolled in the same vocational subjects. One Friday afternoon, Mohammad who studies in the same school wanted to walk home with Ayesha who in turn asked Haridja to come with them. Haridja refused and went ahead to hide that she felt hurt. At home, she cried to her mother saying, " Ayesha does not want to be my friend any more. She walked home with Mohammad."

Haridja's mother explained to her that in order to keep friends, she should let her friends have other friends. Her mother made her understand that it is natural for a girl in her teens to begin to get interested in the opposite sex. The next year, Haridja found this to be true.

Guide questions for discussion:

1. Do you know of a group of friends who broke up their friendship because some of the members became interested in the other sex?
2. If you belong to such a group, and are starting to be interested in the opposite sex, how will you deal with your friends who do not feel the same way as you do?
3. If you are not yet interested in the opposite sex, how will you behave toward your friends who are starting to be interested in members of the opposite sex? Should you break up your friendship with them? Why?

Situation No.3

A group of boys are resting under the shade of a tree on the school-ground. They have just sweated out one game of basketball. Yusop, the prankster, teases Usman as he spots Halima from a distance. Usman blushes and returns the teasing, this time directing it at Omar, who caught unaware, stands up and angrily throws the ball at Usman. Ayub pacifies Omar. He tells them that there is really nothing to be mad about since all of them have "secret loves".

Guide questions for discussion:

1. Was Omar right in getting angry at Usman?
2. Have you ever been teased about being secretly in love with somebody? How did you feel ?
3. Was Ayub right in saying that there is really nothing to be mad about as all of them have "secret loves"?

Situation No.4

Mariam is in high spirits again. She hums happily as she walks to the next class. She will be seeing her favourite Math teacher. How she admires his lowpitched and well-modulated voice, his neat appearance from head to foot, and his towering 5´9" stature! Her mother once or twice scolded her for coming home late from school. Actually, those were the times she waited for her favourite Math teacher to be able to talk to him.

Guide question for discussion:

1. What can you say about Mariam's behaviour? Is she in love or is she just admiring her teacher?
2. Have you ever experienced the same feeling? Have you heard of other having such an experience?
3. Is this experience natural for young people?
4. What may be some reasons for Mariam's attraction to her Math teacher?
5. What do you call this attraction toward or admiration for an older person?

After the class discussion on the various situations, proceed to a summary discussion by groups. Divide the class in to 4 or 5 groups. Lead the groups to discuss the following:

1. Define or explain the term *sex drive.*
2. From the situations discussed, what are the manifestations of the sex drive? What other manifestations of the sex drive have you observed?
3. Will all boys and girls develop or have sex drives?
4. What emotional problems are related to the sex drive? Suggest ways of solving these problems.

After the buzz sessions, have each group report on the results of its discussion.

SUGGESTED ACTIVITY 2.1.2

Forum Discussion

1. Organize a forum discussion, participated in by a parent to represent the views of the home; a community leader, the captain, or the president of a civic organization to rep-

resent the views of society in general; a priest, minister, or imam or the three of them or their representatives to represent the views of different religions; and a student leader to offer several points of view on the matter of sexual behaviour. These invited speakers should be informed in advance of what they are supposed to discuss. A committee of students should be formed to invite these people. Aside from the speakers, there should also be a moderator who may be one representing the community. He may be the classroom teacher or a class leader.

2. The forum speakers and the moderator sit in front of the audience or class. The leader introduces the topic and the speakers. When presenting his side of the topic for class consideration, the speaker stands in front of the class. There is no questioning or debating among the speakers themselves as in the case of a panel discussion. Instead, the time is given over to the class to direct the questions to the different speakers after all of them have finished their turns and expressed their personal opinions about the issue.

3. At the end of the open forum, the moderator sees to it that a summary of the pertinent remarks by the forum speakers and the class is given. He may either give the summary himself, lead the speakers into giving the summary, or, he may arrange for a group from the class to make the summary.

4. After the speakers have left, ask the class for conflicting views, or differences of opinions, expressed by the different speakers. Ask the students what they think about these inconsistencies. Tell them:

"You have expressed your views and feelings regarding the sex drives. We have discussed the views of the home, peers, church, and community regarding the different types of sex drives. Sex drives or urges are normal and healthy. They are as common and as natural as eating and sleeping, as being born and dying. The intensity or strength of the sex drives varies considerably from individual to individual and from age to age. There is nothing "wrong" or "dirty" about the sex drives, however, they should be controlled and

guided. Why should the sex drives be controlled and guided?"

5. Encourage the students to probe further on their views that if the sex urges will be allowed unchecked, they might result in the following consequences:

   1. Mental anxiety or conflict
   2. Loss of self-respect
   3. loss of social acceptance
   4. early and forced marriages
   5. venereal diseases
   6. etc.

6. Ask the students about the effects of mental anxiety and loss of self-respect on one's physical and mental health. Ask them further about the possible effects of early and forced marriages and venereal diseases on one's physical and mental health.

7. Impress on the students the fact that as adolescents they might feel quite capable of expressing physical love, but emotionally and psychologically, they still lack the long preparation that is needed to assume or accept the responsibility and consequences of the relationships they will undertake with the opposite sex.

SUGGESTED ACTIVITY 2.1.3

Appropriate Sexual Behaviour

A. Have five columns on the chalkboard labelled as follows:

   1. Appropriate for children
   2. Appropriate for teenagers at all times
   3. Sometimes appropriate for teenagers
   4. Appropriate for adults
   5. Never appropriate

B. Have these phrases written on small pieces of paper, then roll and place them in a box or in a jar.

1. Kisses mother at home.
2. Kisses father at home.
3. kisses father in public
4. Kisses mother in public
5. Cries if hurt
6. does not cry in public
7. holds hands with the opposite sex in public
8. walks down the street with arm around partner
9. hits back if hit
10. joins group in stoning the school windows
11. talks freely with opposite sex
12. dresses to attract opposite sex
13. dates with the opposite sex
14. obeys parents
15. engages in petting
16. dresses sloppily
17. wishes to have friends of the opposite sex
18. flirts with the opposite sex
19. argues about points he does not agree with
20. competes to win
21. Plays truant in school
22. talks against friends behind their back
23. smokes
24. kisses date in a movie house

25. dates different partners
26. masturbates or fondles one's genitals
27. gambles in public places
28. dances the modern dance
29. wears a swimming suit
30. wears clothes that belong to the opposite sex
31. drinks hard drinks
32. takes drugs

Ask students to write each phrase under the column where it belongs. Have the students examine the list they have made. Ask them if they all agree, more or less, with the list. If they list most of the phrases under the sometimes category, this indicates that they are in the transition stage from childhood to adolescence and reflects the kind of values they have or seem to favour. They are not yet sure of the code of behaviour they want to follow. The result of this list, although limited, points out the aspects of the code that need emphasis.

Suggested Activity 2.1.4

The teacher asks the class this question: What is right and what is wrong?

Provide for a free-wheeling discussion. Then present these situations for the reaction of the class.

Situation 1

You were finally admitted to a gang which you have wanted to join for a long time. As days pass, you begin to disagree with some of the practices of the gang, like cutting classes when the lesson is not interesting or smoking marijuana. As a member, you are supposed to do as the rest do but you have been trained in self-discipline by your parents.

Guide questions for discussion:

a) What is the conflict in this situation?

b) What are the alternatives? Between these alternatives, is there a better choice?:

c) What is the right thing to do?

Situation 2

Faisal was invited by his friends to a jam session. He did not tell his mother about it because he knew his mother wouldn't allow him to attend jam sessions on school days. he cut his afternoon class to attend the jam session. He reached home much later then usual. When asked by his mother, Faisal said that he came late because the bus he took broke down.

Guide questions for discussion:

a) Did Faisal do right? Why not?

b) What would you have done if you were in his place?

Situation 3

One Friday afternoon, Rose and her best friend, Rory, went foursome with their classmates, Andy and Tony, to see a movie. They skipped their physical Education classes. When they were leaving the movie house, they met Gloria, Rose's older sister who is in senior high, with her boyfriend. Rose felt uneasy and scared.

Guide questions for discussion:

a) What are the conflicts in the situation?

b) What are the alternatives for Rose?

c) If you were Rose, what would you do? Why?

Situation 4

Muslims are obliged to attend the Wajib or Friday prayers. They are forbidden to watch pomography (Haram).

Faisal and Abdul were on their way to the Wajib for the Friday Sermon (Khutbah) when they met some classmates who invited them to see a pornographic movie.

Guide questions for discussion:

a) What is the conflict in this situation?

b) What are the alternatives?

c) If you were Abdul or Faisal, what would you do? Why?

After the above discussions the teacher asks: What is right and what is wrong? What are the possible consequences of right and wrong decisions? The students may give answers similar to the following:

Right actions, decisions, and attitudes produce:

1. increased trust among people.
2. greater integrity in relationships.
3. dissolution of barriers separating people.
4. co-operation
5. enhanced self-respect.
6. an appreciation of personal worth.

Wrong actions, decisions, and attitudes produce:

1. mistrust of people.
2. disloyalty in relationship.
3. conflict between persons and groups.
4. resistance and non-cooperation.
5. loss of self-respect.
6. dishonesty.

Every person is subject to the basic rules of moral conduct expected by society. Conflicts arise when one's values and experiences differ from the expectations of society. A person can help resolve conflicts by using inner direction in making decisions on the morality or immorality of his sex behaviour. Our sex behaviour is judged moral or immoral according to the cultural values of the people. Any departure from the accepted values of our culture or group to which we belong becomes immoral. Moral values include such traits as responsibility, love and mutual respect, discipline, justice and fairness, religious faith, co-operation, faithfulness, and filial love.

Intended message: Teenagers should have a code or standard of right and wrong to help them decide about present or future sexual behaviour.

SUGGESTED ACTIVITY 2.1.5

Here are some situations teenagers may find themselves in now or in the future. Let them describe briefly what they will do in each of these situations.

Situation 1

You have very strict parents. They do not allow you to join social activities at school.

Situation 2

Your friends at school decide to try smoking marijuana. You know your father does not approve of this. "Smoking is bad for the health", he says.

Situation 3

Your parents do not allow you to entertain suitors at home. they say that you are too young to be entertaining suitors and that your primary interest should be your studies.

Situation 4

There is someone in your neighbourhood you have a "crush" on. All you think about is your "crush". You can't seem to do anything except to swoon over this boy/girl. Unfortunately, the object of your "crush" doesn't even know you exist. This has affected your grades as well as your appetite adversely.

Situation 5

Some of your friends go to the park with their boy/girl friends for a stroll. You have heard about what boys and girls do when they are in the park—they kiss, neck, and even pet. Your boy/girl friend is inviting you to take a walk in the same park.

Situation 6

You are on your way to a Wajib (Friday prayer). You meet some friends who invite you to join them to see a pornographic movie.

Situation 7

As a Muslim girl, you are not allowed to leave the house unchaperoned. one beautiful night, a boy in your class invites you for a stroll along the beach.

2.2. SEXUALITY IN CHILDHOOD AND ADOLESCENCE

Objectives :

1. To discuss the development of sexuality from childhood to adolescence.
2. To differentiate between pregenital and genital sexuality.
3. To identify specific behaviours that adolescents exhibit during social and emotional maturation or development.
4. To discuss various problems of adolescents and to offer solutions to these problems.

Time Required : 60 minutes

Materials : Information Sheets

PROCEDURE

1. Present a lecture based on the Information Sheet given in this lesson.
2. After the lecture, have students do the activities and exercises given at the end of this lesson.

SUGGESTED ACTIVITY 2.2.1

Below is a list of changes that are experienced by an adolescent. Write S to indicate a sexual change; E, an emotional change; and SD, a social development change.

________ 1. Characterized by "narcissism" in which erotic interest is expressed toward persons very much like the self.

________ 2. During adolescence, the peer group influence is greater than that of parents.

________ 3. Love is the dominant feeling of the adolescent.

________ 4. When adolescent interests are not expressed in reality, they usually appear in day-dreams, wishes and imagination.

________ 5. In adolescence, pregenital erogenous zones are second to the genital zone as the primary source of sexual excitement.

________ 6. The genital urges are primarily gratified in fact/ in fantasy, through the opposite sex.

________ 7. Authoritarian discipline, including physical punishment, is associated with dependency/rebelliousness in adolescents.

Discussion Points

1. What are some of the delinquent offenses committed by adolescents?
2. What are the factors associated with delinquency among adolescents?
3. What other psychological problems are experienced by some adolescents?

INFORMATION SHEET

The sexual instincts of human beings are, according to Freud, the father of psychoanalysis, at their peak during the adolescence. He classified the development of psycho-sexual instinct under two broad phases- the pregenital sexuality and the genital sexuality.

Pregenital sexuality

In the pregenital sexuality, during the first year of life, the region around the infant's mouth-similar to all erogenous zones, is the primary source of sexual instinct. Gratification of this instinct is accomplished through sucking the mother's breast, the child's own thumbs or other suckable objects.

Between the ages 1 and 3, the primary erogenous zone is the anal region. Again, the child derives sexual pleasure from this region of the body, especially during defecation. This oral and anal genital sexuality does not differ for boys and girls. Not until the first stage of gentility, the Oedipal period (3 to 5 years of age) does psycho-sexual development diverge for the two genders.

Genital sexuality

Between the ages of 3 and 5 (the Oedipal period), the primary source of sexual excitation originates from the genital region, defining the first stage of genital sexuality, accompanied by strong feelings of sexual attraction to the parent of the opposite sex as an abject for gratification.

Psychosexual development diverges in important ways for boys and girls during the Oedipal stage. Both boys and girls are sexually attracted to the parent of the opposite sex, and as a result they experience frustration and anxiety. Boys develop Oedipus complex and girls Electra complex. Frustration and anxiety intensify throughout this stage of development. Finally, the child must make use of psychological defenses against these negative emotions through identifying with the same sex parent, internalizing their parent's value system, and expressing their sexual impulses, which characterize the later childhood years, which Freud referred to as the stage of latency.

A series of transformations take place during the adolescent period that lead to adult heterosexual functioning. One very important transformation is the transition from infantile sexuality to normal genital sexuality.

"With the beginning of puberty, changes set in which transform the infantile sexual ape into its definite normal form"(Freud 1905/1962).

In adolescence, pregenital erogenous zones become subordinate to the genital zone as the primary source of sexual excitation. For most adults, primary gratification is obtained through the genital erogenous zones during heterosexual intercourse.

A second transformation occurring during the adolescent period is the change from a primarily autocratic or masturbatory sexual impulse to an impulse which is directed towards an external object. There are several adolescent phases of sexuality different before the final phase of heterosexual sexuality is reached. Early adolescence is characterized by "Narcissism" in which erotic interest is directed toward the self as well as toward persons very much like the self.

Freud's Psychosexual Stages

Stage	Age	Major characteristics
Oral	Birth-1	Mouth region is the primary erogenous zone; sucking for gratification; relative primary of the id—the unconscious part of our consciousness, instincts, urges etc.
Anal	1-3	Anus is the primary erogenous zone; def ecation as form of gratification; feces as gifts; ego as aid in adaptation of external reality.
Oedipal	3-5	Bcys: Penis as source of sexual excitations; incestuous fantasies toward mother and rivalry with father; culminating in intense castration anxiety and sexual repression. At this stage the *super ego* - the part of our consciousness which reflects society's and authorities' expectations, norms and values develops. Girls: Clitoris as source of sexual excitation; anatomical enlightenment leads to castration complex (feeling that she has been castrated and is inferior to boys), culminating in repression of sexual instincts.
Latency	5-Puberty	Period of sexual repression during which the *ego* the part of our consciousness which balances the demands of the id and the super ego and which is considered a person's identity or soul becomes significantly strengthened.
Adult Genital	Adolescence 12-19	Development of sex-role, identification & choice of non-incenstuous heterosexual object choice.

Establishment of psychological autonomy, and breaking away from parental authority is the third transition in psychosexual identity in adolescence. The process through which a person develops psychological autonomy from parents and the emergence of an independent identity is often referred to as "individuation".

The homosexual love, the so-called narcissistic friendships often contain an erotic component that may be expressed in overt behaviour such as mutual masturbation during puberty. The heterosexual identity (love towards opposite sex) becomes clearly patterned in late adolescence. Although they have achieved psychosexual identity, adolescents may not experience heterosexual intercourse. Still, genital urges are primarily gratified in fact in fantasy, through the opposite sex.

Children at this age can develop many complexes due to premature indulgence in sex or sudden repression of the same. Formation of mental complexes due to self-abuse and other different forms of erotic behaviur can give rise to mental phobias, anxiety neurosis, melancholia in which the individual is haunted by a sense of sin and thinks himself lost beyond redemption. Thus the lack of proper education leads the young soul into great mental agony and suffering. Abuse of sex is the roof of juvenile faults, immoralities, and crime. Moderate work and music, early rising, proper use of sex energy in creative works outdoor games, sports, cocurricular activities, scout and guide training etc. are helpful in self-control and cures the habit of self-abuse. A balance between freedom and control helps the adolescent to natural development and self-discipline. Sex enlightenment provided through the schools as regular subjects of the curriculum helps the adolescents to understand the nature of different phenomena. Adolescents' curiosity about sex is satisfied by providing orientation in an objective and unbiased manner. According to some writers, co-education improves sex morality among boys and girls.

SOCIAL DEVELOPMENT AND PARENTAL AUTHORITY

The relationship between adolescents and their parents involves reciprocal influence, particularly in the area of discipline. Generally authoritarian discipline, including physical punishment, promotes dependency and rebelliousness in adolescents. Highly permissive discipline may also lead to dependency. With physical maturation in puberty, adolescents become more assertive in relating with their parents.

Contrary to the implications of the term 'generation gap' research reveals few dramatic differences between attitudes and values of adolescents and their parents. Adolescents attribute more positive characteristics to adults than they do to adolescents although the peer group influence is greater than that of parents. During this time, adolescent attitudes toward parents become less favourable, and their willingness to endorse peer misconduct increases.

Evidence from research suggests that adolescents show increasing autonomy with age; they become somewhat less likely to conform to either parents or to peers as they grow older. Conformity to antisocial behaviour peaks in middle-adolescence at around age 15, but in general they are less likely to conform to antisocial behaviour than to presocial or neutral behaviour.

According to Sullivan's theory, the major interpersonal need systems of security, intimacy, and lust come into conflict in adolescents. Separation from parents has positive psychological effects for both adolescents and their parents. A greater degree of separation show more independence from, and affection toward,their parents.

Emotional development

Adolescence is a period of great excitability and turbulent emotions. Love is the dominant feeling of the adolescence. The early interests of adolescents are personal in nature; but the social and emotional changes that appear at this stage are reflected in the development of interests in others and especially a changed attribute and feeling toward members of the opposite sex. The play life of adolescents involves more of the team spirit and group action then was the case during the pre-adolescent stage. Adolescent boys continue to show an interest in adventure, but adventures are less fantastic and are more closely connected with present day living conditions and problems.

When adolescents interests are not expressed in reality they usually appear in day dreams wishes and imagination. It is essential that parents and teachers have a knowledge of an adolescent's interests, so that they may aid him/her better to understand himself/herself and direct or guide him/her toward a more complete fulfillment of his/her aspirations and possibilities. It is the prime duty of the educator to see that adolescents feeling of love does not take some mischievous turn. Adolescent love is to be utilized in the service of society. It should not be allowed to waste itself away in mere vituperations of the heart.

Juvenile delinquency

The distinction between delinquent behaviour and official delinquency is important. 'Delinquent behaviour' refers to any act of a juvenile that would be a chargeable offence according to juvenile justice/laws. 'Official delinquency' refers to those acts by adolescents for which they are actually apprehended for delinquent behaviour. The disparity between these two categories, acts performed but not resulting in legal action, is referred to as 'hidden delinquency'.

The term 'delinquency' is derived from a latin word meaning "to leave undone". It is defined by Webster's New World Dictionary as "failure or neglect to do what duty or law requires". The term is usually preceded by the word "juvenile", so as to limit its application to adolescents (and in exceptional cases, to children). In practice, delinquency usually refers to acts committed by youth in willful violation of rules or statutes. Juvenile behaviour includes instances of undetected or hidden delinquency, as well as cases of official juvenile delinquency. These delinquent offenses may be as follows:

- Violation of law or ordinance
- Habitual truancy
- Association with known thieves, vicious or immoral persons
- Incorrigibility
- being beyond control of parents or guardian
- Growing up in idleness or crime

- Injuring self or others
- Immoral or indecent conduct
- Absence from home without parents' or guardian's consent
- Habitual use of vile, obscene, or vulgar language
- Visits to houses of ill repute
- Habitual wandering
- Jumping train or entering car without authority
- Patronizing shop where intoxicating liquor is sold
- Wandering streets at night
- Immoral conduct
- Smoking cigarettes or using tobacco
- Addiction to drugs
- Disorderly conduct
- Begging
- Use of intoxicating liquor
- Sexual irregularities, etc.

FACTORS ASSOCIATED WITH DELINQUENCY

a) The home

There is direct casual connection between broken homes and delinquency. Adolescents from broken homes or disorganized families have negative attitudes towards their parents. When the relationship between parents and adolescents are strained, the adolescents are more likely to become official delinquents which in turn is likely to cause some deterioration in family relationship.

b) Social class

Many people assume that lower-class adolescents are more likely to engage in delinquent behaviour than their middle and upper-class counterparts. A study found no significant difference between lower-class gang and non-gang, lower-class and middle-class boys in the evaluation of the middle-class norms. However, a study by Empey and Erickson (1965) showed a slight tendency for the upper-class boys to commit fewer delinquent act than the boys in the two groups.

On the other hand, arrest rates for juvenile delinquency do show a strong tendency to be higher among lower class adolescents. This may be due to the possibility of bias in arrest rates as a function of class and race.

c) Intelligence

Studies on the relationship between delinquent behaviour on the one hand, and social class or race, on the other, indicate that overall delinquent behavior is a function of racial and socio-economic groupings. Intelligence also seems to exert an influence on delinquent behaviour. Adolescents with lower I.Q. are more likely to exhibit delinquent behaviour. Education attainment is associated with juvenile delinquency. High school drop-outs have been found to be involved in serious delinquency.

DELINQUENCY AMONG GIRLS

While the young male delinquent shows a wide variety of behaviour, the girl, in contrast, possesses a quite limited delinquent repertoire. By and large, her legally defined offences consists of sexual acting, vagrancy, running away, and stealing.

Adolescent girls commit a full range of delinquent acts, not specializing in any given category. They are far less likely than males, however, to engage in theft of large amounts, gang fist fights, gambling or promiscuous sexual behaviour .

Each of the factors that have been cited above-family relationships, social class, age intelligence education housing-equally affect males and females. Broken homes have equally harmful effects on adolescent boys and girls. It is certainly possible that sex-role consolidation in adolescence is a process heavily influenced by environmental contexts, such as family situation and socio-economic status.

PSYCHOLOGICAL PROBLEMS OF ADOLESCENTS

Adolescent schizophrenia

Schizophrenia is only one diagnostic category for psychiatric problems in adolescence. Schizophrenia is a serious psychological disorder that is characterized by an inability to function in the day-to-day world. It includes marked impairment in intellectual functioning, bizarre thought processes, such as delusions and hallucinations and little or no awareness of the disorder. Schizophrenia accounts for approximately 8-10 per cent of cases of psychological problems in adolescence. The onset of schizophrenia may appear in childhood or early adolescence, prior to onset of the disorder. Approximately one-third to one-half of preschizophrenic adolescents are identifiable as " deviant" during childhood. The likelihood of making a good adjustment is poorer for adolescent schizophrenics than it is for adolescents with other psychiatric problems. Prognosis is poorer for younger than for older adolescents.

Depression and suicide

Depression is a relatively rare diagnosis among adolescents, although it may be a common psychological experience. Behavioural manifestations of depression include drug abuse, alcohol abuse, promiscuity, and suicide attempts. Suicidal behaviour among adolescents is accompanied by serious depression in about 80 per cent of cases. Many psychologists believe that alienation may be a mediating factor in adolescent suicidal behaviour. Several studies have suggested that family problems are also important contributing factors.

Suicidal adolescents show evidence of disordered thinking. They appear to be more rapid thinkers who refuse to consider alternative solutions, and appear to view the world dichotomously, that is: admitting no compromises between happiness and despair.

Use of drugs and alcohol

A larger percentage of adolescents now use alcohol and drugs than previously. A substantial proportion of high-school and higher secondary school students, particularly males are problem drinkers. Drinking among adolescents often is associated with family problems, frustration in love, parental separation and parental alcoholism.

Achieving heterosexuality

From self-love or narcisism over homosexuality the adolescent finally moves to heterosexuality. Heterosexuality, however, can pose many problems among adolescents. If the environment contains a large number of potential mates it can be easy and natural. But adolescents are often too shy to make the necessary social contacts. They may have actual or fancied deformities which allow them to imagine themselves as unattractive. Or they may have experienced some great sexual shock and have become too inhibited ever to react normally.

Girls who have strong feelings of rivalry with boys may be unable ever to fall in love with them. Boys with strong fixations on their mothers may be likewise be unable to fall in love with any other female. Some boys may be too suspicious of girls to love any of them and thus, boys and girls may regress to homosexual love.

The effect of sexual ignorance

Ignorance and misinformation often lead to illegitimacy, rape, and veneral diseases or sexual crimes among adolescents. More common but not less important are the emotional bruises that may attend the unprepared adolescent's first sexual experience.

Adolescent masturbation

About 70 to 90 per cent of boys and from 30 to 70 per cent of females admit to having masturbated during adolescence. Organically, there is no difference between masturbation and sexual intercourse. Masturbation, therefore, has no unique physical effects on the mind or body. The adolescent masturbator will not loose his virility, become a pervert, or loose his intellect because of this practice. But excess of everything is bad. As far as possible the sex energy should be sublimated by creative works, sports, games, artistic activities and other cocurricular activities, religious pursuits, social work etc.

Becoming independent of the family, attaining emotional

and social maturity are concerns of adolescence which should be attained through social interaction. Proper guidance should be provided by the parents and teachers. Keeping in view that so many emotional, psychosexual tensions, conflicts, guilt and anxiety are experienced during adolescence, it is truly called " a period of storm and stress".

2.3 LOVE

Objectives :

1 To understand the concept of love and the different types of love.

2. To differentiate between mature and immature love.

3. To list ways of showing love to one's parents, friends, girlfriend/boyfriend.

Time Required : 120 minutes

Materials : Information Sheet, blackboard, newsprint, marker pen.

PROCEDURE

1. Ask the students to explain what "love" is.
2. Distribute blank writing sheets.
3. Ask the students to list ways of showing their lov· for their:
   a) parents/family
   b) friends
   c) boy friend/girl friend
4. Discuss the following points:-
   a) Were the couple in love?
   b) Do you think they should have married?
      If yes, why? If no, why not?
   c) Could they have sustained the relationship without

getting married?

5. Distribute the Handout: Information Sheet: "Mature and Immature Love".

6. Discuss the definition of the different types of love based on Sol Gordon's in definition in the Information Sheet: "What is love".

7. If time permits distribute the case studies to the students and use the case studies for further discussion. Refer to Teacher's Note for answers.

INFORMATION SHEET

What is Love?

Love is sharing. Love is action. Love is caring. Love has to be demonstrated through deeds and action. Love needs time and sacrifice. If we cannot love we can't expect to be loved. Love does not mean total agreement in all issues.

Love is the predominant factor that creates and holds them together. Love like electricity can be described by its results but it is hard to pin down exactly what it is. We can also love many people in different ways and show our love in varying degrees to different people.

Love is not just a feeling but a relationship. Love is only meaningful when it is expressed in action. It may be expressed in various forms depending on the person we love. Love is a commitment. Love is energizing rather then exhausting.

Sol Gordon has this to say about love. Being "in love" usually refers to a powerful desire to be with and to please another person. When you are in love, you will be eager to win not only the affection but the respect of the other person. You will want him or her to be proud of you in as many ways as possible. Young people sometimes say (and believe) that they are in love, but then act in a way that is calculated to undermine the relationship. They may neglect their studies or their work; they may be careless about their appearance; they may neglect their studies or their work; they may be careless about their appearance; they may be jealous, or irritable, or petty when they are with the other person; they may fail to keep promises or to assume obligations that are taken for granted when people really love each other. Such a pattern of behaviour makes it quite clear that while there maybe a strong attraction between a young man or woman the relationship is far too immature to be considered love. People who are truly in love will be so intent on making themselves the best possible partner for their loved one that they will be inspired to improve their work, to enhance their appearance, and to bring out the best side of their personality. They express their love in short by trying in every way possible to make themselves better persons so that they will be more worthy of the love that they want to receive.

Different types of love

a) Love for parents.

b) Love among siblings

c) Love for friends.

d) Conjugal love.

MATURE AND IMMATURE LOVE

How can you tell if you are really in love? There are many ways of interpreting this emotional relationship and of assessing it in particular instances. It may be helpful to start out by distinguishing two types of involvement which come under the general heading of "love" although they are very different from each other.

Mature love

Mature love prevails when your caring about the other person is just a little bit more important to you than having the other person care for you. This kind of relationship is mutually enhancing and energizing. In other words, it makes both partners feel better, not only in a few peak moments but also in the difficult business of day-to-day living.

Immature love

Immature love prevails when it is much more important to have the other person care for you than it is for you to care for the other person. This kind of relationship is often perceived as more of burden than a privilege. Since it involves more taking than giving, it tends to be emotionally exhausting.

In marriage, as in other relationships, communication is often blocked. There are innumerable ways in which this may occur, differing widely from person to person and from couple to couple. Here are just a few more or less typical instances.

a) You want to say something to your partner but you hold off because you're afraid that you will hurt his or her feelings. You assume that the other person can't take it. But your assumptions may be quite wrong, and you may miss an opportunity to bring out something important to both of you.

b) Instead of speaking directly to your partner about some matter that concerns you, you talk to a mutual friend, or to a parent, or to an inlaw. By the time you've finished spilling everything into these sympathetic ears, you may have lost the intense desire to convey your message directly to the person involved- to get it off your chest. If the message eventually reaches your partner, it may well be distorted. Also the partner may resent being reached indirectly and being " the last to know".

c) You may complain to your partner about some relatively small matter when there is really something much more important on your mind. For example, when a wife reproaches her husband for forgetting her birthday, when what she really means is that he hasn't been paying enough attention to her recently.

No one instance of failure or blocking of communication between marriage partners is likely to be too serious, but the overall effect, if it continues for a long time, may well be disastrous. The partners must make a conscious effort to overcome these barriers and to "get through" to each other. This isn't easy and may require frequent reminders on both sides. Sometimes a more open attitude goes against the grain of long-established habits. Spontaneity and mutual confidence will develop as the man and woman become more comfortable with each other.

SUGGESTED ACTIVITY 2.3.1

Development of Love

The following case studies can be used as discussion starters by posing the question: How will you solve the problem?

Case study I

Q. I am a 17-yearold girl. A few months back, at a party, I met a boy who is a year older. We went out often for several months and I got to know him pretty well. I think I am in love with him but I´am not sure.

Last week, he asked me for a kiss but I refused. Since then, he has repeatedly asked me but I never gave in to his wish. I know that if I do, it'll lead to something deeper. But if I don't, he may drop me.

I can´t bear to lose him. I think I'll give in to him if he asks me again. Please answer me as soon as possible as I need guidance. My parents do not know about this and I don't feel like telling them.

Case study 2

Q. I am in my middle teens. I love a boy in my school who is a year older and is very handsome. He is of a different religion and race. The problem is that I am too shy to talk to him. We have never talked to each other. Three weeks ago, he asked for my address through his friend, but I didn't give it because I was too shy and afraid he would write letters to me. I want to know what he feels for me. How will I start the conversion. Please help me, I love him so much. I'm going crazy over him. I can't sleep well at night thinking about him.

Case Study 3

Q. I am a boy, aged 16. Recently I told my mother that I am in love with a girl in school. My mother said I was crazy. She said a young boy like me would not understand what love is. She also said love could only be understood by an adult.

She told me that mine was a case of puppy love. I thought about all that and decided to tell my girlfriend.

My girlfriend was very upset when she heard this. She asked her mother about it and her mother said it might be true.

Now Iam very upset. Would you please tell me what "puppy love" is and what is true love? I love her and have real feelings for her. She also feels the same way.

Case study 4

Q. I am a 13-year-old girl and I am in love with a boy who is 15 yearold. We love each other. One night he asked me to go out with him and we went to a coffee house near our school. The next day I told my parents I wanted to get married to him. When my father heard about this he slapped me. I love my boyfriend very much. Please tell me what to do.

Teacher's notes:

Case study 1

A. If the only way you can keep a boy is to go against your own values, is he worth keeping? Why don't you trust him a little more? Believe that he will respect your feelings and your moral standards; talk to him about the dilemma he puts you in. You probably won't lose him after all.

You should also examine this fear you have that a kiss will inevitably lead to something more. You both have control over what you do-you are not dealing with an irresistible, fatal force. If you both decide on the limits, you can keep them.

Case study 2

A. You can't have it both ways. Either you want to get to know him or you don't. If you do, then you have to give him an opening, like giving him your address or phone number or a chance to talk to you in a group. So many girls reject the approaches made by boys they actually like because they are "shy" or "proud", or think that is the only correct way to behave. As a result, they are in great distress when the boys give up trying.

Case study 3

A. The love you feel is real enough. It is possibly more intense than the love your mother feels for your father. But it is different from adult love several ways. It is most unlikely that in in 10 years' time you will still love her. Adolescents change so fast that in six months you may wonder what on earth you saw in her.

Adult love carries with it responsibilities which you are not ready to handle now, including a commitment to share your life with someone and create a home and family. But just because love will not last does not mean that it is not serious. Young love is just as serious as going to school, which is a preparation for adult working life.

Teenagers are very romantic and sometimes they fall in love for pretty trivial reasons, such as the hero status of being a sports star, or the attraction of long hair. Many teenagers, especially girls, are also so lonely and eager for love that they imagine a marvellous collection of good qualities being present in their current boyfriends. Several months later, the rosy clouds blow away and she sees a bad-tempered boy with acne.

But it is only through your experience of people, while you are growing up, that you are able to become an adult who can truly perceive the good and bad qualities of a person. It takes a mature couple to see realistically whether they share enough of the same values and goals to make a happy marriage. There are many adults around who have yet to learn this.

Case study 4

A. Your father shouldn't have slapped you, but it is not really very surprising that he lost control of himself. Suddenly his 13-year-old baby girl, hardly into puberty, is thinking of getting married. You yourself know that is pretty silly. You are still in school.

It will be five years before you reach the legal age to marry and then another three years before you can marry without your father's consent. Eight years altogether. Do you think your relationship with your boyfriend will last that long?

Sure, you like him very much; he is a very special friend. But that means you like to see him, talk to him, and feel that he cares about you. It doesn't mean that you are ready to be a wife and mother. Don't give your poor father any more shocks. Let him slowly get used to the idea that you are becoming a woman.

2.4 DATING AND RELATIONSHIP

Objectives :

1. To understand the various dating customs throughout the world.
2. To define what dating is and identify the objectives of dating.
3. To study various attitudes towards dating.
4. To identify what is an ideal dating partner.
5. To solve problems on dating.

Time Required : 30-45 minutes

Materials : Handout and felt pens

PROCEDURE

1. There is no informational outline for this section because students are the best source of information on current dating customs. A lecture, however, can present a histori-

cal/anthropological picture of dating customs throughout the world. It will be interesting to present some examples of anthropological case studies of dating customs, and then have the students come up with an "anthropological" study of the dating customs in their school. Let the students educate you.

2. One of the main purposes of this section is to allow the class to share information in a group and to help them clarify the nature of dating and the reasons for it. Talk about the purpose of "dating" and discuss issues that are important to the students. Do not automatically assume that sex is an issue. Remember that dating may not even be of interest or concern to some students.

SUGGESTED ACTIVITY 2.4.1

Discussion questions

1. *How does a person decide whom to go out with?*
2. *What do young people do when they go out? Where do they go?*
3. *When is a person old enough to date?*
4. *What does it mean "to date"? Do young people still date?*
5. *Should planning and paying for dates be the male's responsibility?*
6. *Do adolescents go steady? Should they?*
7. *How would you define a good relationship?*
8. *What qualities in a girl does a boy admire?*
9. *What qualities in a boy does a girl admire?*
10. *For what reasons should a person get married?*
11. *How does a person know when he/she is ready to get married?*
12. *What are some of the problems that might happen in a marriage?*

13. *Are there any differences between traditional marriages and modern marriages?*

14. *Ask the boys: How would you react if a girl you know only by sight came up to you after class and asked you to go to the movie with her?*

15. *Ask the girls: Would you feel comfortable asking a boy you know only by sight to go to the movies? Why or why not?*

16. *If a boy pays for the date, does he expect something in return? What do girls think boys expect? What do boys actually expect?*

SUGGESTED ACTIVITY 2.4.2

Incomplete Sentences

Dating is................................
Romance is................................
Love is................................
Going steady is................................
Boys shouldn't date girls who................................
Girls shouldn't date boys who................................
Girls who ask boys out are................................
Marriage is................................
Divorce is................................
Living with the same person for the rest of my life would be.....................
The different between living together and marriage is.............................
Teenagers who marry are................................

SUGGESTED ACTIVITY 2.4.3

Continuums/Values Voting

1. A 16-year-old girl should be allowed to stay out on a date for as long as she wishes.

2. A 16-year-old boy should be allowed to stay out on a date for as long as he wishes.

3. Parents should have a voice in deciding with whom their

children go out.

4. The boy should ask the girl to go out, not vice versa.
5. They boy should pay for the date.
6. A person should live with his/her partner before they get married.
7. Virginity until marriage is a value that is not out of date.

SUGGESTED ACTIVITY 2.4.4

Desirable Qualities in a Boy/Girlfriend

In this exercise the students will look closely at the range of qualities they desire in a prospective boyfriend/girlfriend. Because it can be done anonymously, the exercise allows students to respond from their own personal opinions rather than from peer pressure.

PROCEDURE

1. Provide each of the students with a list of desired personal characteristics of a potential boyfriend/girfriend. Ask them to rank the characteristics in their order of importance. Tell them that this is an anonymous poll and that only the total group scores will be made known. Instruct students not to write their names on the paper. Have them indicate only whether they are male or female.

   a) Good looks
   b) Intelligence
   c) Fair, willing to share unpleasant tasks
   d) Same race
   e) Well-off financially
   f) Sports-mind
   g) Warm and affectionate
   h) Honest and sensitive
   i) Good sense of humour

j) Good health

k) Sexually responsive

l) Good housekeeper

m) Good cook

n) Virgin

o) Desire for children

p) Other (specify)

2. (Optional) Hand out another sheet with the same qualities and ask them to rank them in order of what would be the most important for a marriage partner. Or add a second column to rate the qualities of a marriage partner.

3. Collect and tabulate the lists. Separate the male list from the female list in order to compare scores.

4. After tabulation (the next day) present the results. Have the class react to and discuss the results. The students will be very interested in comparing the males' scores with females.' It can also be interesting to discuss the difference in lists for boy/girlfriends versus marriage partners. Talk about the implications of the differences.

Variation

Ask them to have their parents fill out the same list or have the students rank the qualities in terms of how they think their parents would respond. Afterwards have them compare the similarities and differences with their own lists.

Criticisms

Have the students make a list of 10 things which displease them about the opposite sex. (You might want to have the boys and girls separate and come up with a group list). Chart their group responses in the order of frequency and discuss them in the class.

SUGGESTED ACTIVITY 2.4.5

The Ideal Partner

1. Divide the class into two groups: a male and female. Give each group newsprint and a felt pen.

2. Assign each group two tasks.

   a) All the qualities that they would like to have in an ideal boyfriend/girlfriend putting an asterisk beside the three most important ones.

   b) All the qualities that they think the other sex want in an ideal girlfriend/ boyfriend also putting an asterisk beside the three important ones.

3. Allow 10-15 minutes to brainstorm and come up with their lists.

4. Bring the groups back together and have them report on results. Discuss similarities and differences. How accurately did each group perceive the expectations of the opposite sex? If a group is well primed, discussion flows easily.

SUGGESTED ACTIVITY 2.4.6

Letters to the Lovelorn

Ask students to pretend to be counsellors for a day, giving advice to the lovelorn. Distribute the "Letters from the lovelorn" and ask the students to counsel the letter writers.

Discussion Points

1. Were some questions more difficult than others?

2. How do you feel about giving other people advice?

3. How do you feel when people try to give you advice?

4. Would your advice change if you were the one asking the question ? How?

5. How did you use the decision-making process when suggesting a solution?

LETTERS FROM THE LOVELORN

Dear Anh and Tan,

I am a 16-year-old girl. There is a boy in my math class whom I really like, but he doesn't seem to notice me. How can I let him know that I like him?

Invisible Me

Dear Anh and Tan,

I am a 17-year-old. Some of my relatives are concerned that I've never had a real girlfriend. I like girls but I don't know what to say to them. What can I do?

Shy Guy

Dear Anh and Tan,

My boyfriend says that he loves me, but twice I've found out that he has taken another girl out. I get so jealous when I think of him with another girl. What should I do?

Jealous Susan

Dear Anh and Tan,

What can a girl say when turning down a kiss on the first date-especially if she wants the guy to come around again?

Crazy

Dear Anh and Tan,

Some of my friends and I were talking about saying "no". Why is it so much harder to say "no" than "yes"? Sometimes I do not want to accept an invitation but I'm afraid to hurt someone's feelings. What is the best thing to do when your date or the other kids are going somewhere that you know is out of bounds for you. It's always such an awkward situation. What's the best way to say "no"?

Friendly Lady

Dear Anh and Tan,

Which is better, to go to a school dance with a creep or to sit home? I love dances.

Dancing Feet

Dear Anh and Tan,

My dad really pushes me to be athletic. He always wants to go out and play catch or shoot baskets. I'd rather work on my hobbies-painting and playing the guitar. How can I let him know that I don't like sports without hurting his feelings?

Poor Boy

2.5 ADOLESCENT PREGNANCY

Objectives :

1) To discuss the growing number of adolescent pregnancies and the consequences of adolescent pregnancy and parenting both in the pre-marital and marital situations.

2) To explore individual feelings and attitudes about adolescent pregnancy and sexual behaviour.

Time Required : 30-45 minutes

Materials : Information sheet

PROCEDURE

1. Conduct a lecture on adolescent pregnancy, providing information on adolescent sexual behaviour, the number of adolescent pregnancies in various parts of the world, and the consequences of adolescent pregnancy and parenting. The lecture can be based on the Information Sheet.

2. After the lecture, distribute the Information Sheet to the students. Ask them to take the sheet home and discuss the information with their parents.

3. After the lecture, discuss the topics using the discussion points given below.

SUGGESTED ACTIVITY 2.5.1

Discussion Points

1. What do you think it is like to be a teen-age parent both in and out of marriage?
2. What are some of the positive aspects? Negative aspects?
3. Give the effects of early pregnancies on the teen-age mother in terms of medical/health, social, psychological, employment and economic conditions.
4. How does one's life change after parenthood.
5. Compare the early life of a child of a single teenager and the early life of a child of a stable couple in their late 20s.

   Put these two lists on the board for the students to accomplish:

The Benefits of Having a baby	*The problems of Having a baby*
1.	1.
2.	2.
3.	3.
4.	4.

INFORMATION SHEET

Adolescent Pregnancy

There are now signs that the needs of adolescents are gradually being recognized. There is a growing awareness that the number of adolescents is increasing. According to estimates by the United Nation there were 936 million adolescents in 1980 and by the year 2000 this figure will have risen to 1,147 ,million. The period of adolescence is lengthening as biological maturity is reached earlier while social and economic independence is reached later. In addition, sexual activity among adolescents is growing. Another cause for concern is that the trend for births to women under 20 years represents a growing proportion of all births.

Yet the sheer number of adolescents is not the most convincing argument for tackling their reproductive health difficulties. That position is reserved for figures which show the scope of those difficulties. In Indonesia 41 per cent of all women have their first birth before they are 17. And in Panama mothers aged between 15 and 19 accounted for more than a fifth of all births, a study showed. Indeed, although there is still a strong prejudice among old and young in Panama against the use of contraception there are signs that Panamanian parents are beginning to recognize that adolescent sexual behaviour is a problem.

The situation in the developing countries is not well documented but figures such as these give no cause for complacency. Most African and Latin American countries have birth rates of well over 100 per 1,000 for women aged between 15 and 19. For Bangladesh the figure is 203 per 1,000. (This compares with 58 per 1,000 for the United States.) In the Caribbean islands, about 58 percent of first babies are born to mothers aged under 19, and half of those are aged 17 or less. This means a substantial number of young girls become pregnant. In many parts of Africa adolescent pregnancies are reaching epidemic proportions, according to Peris Muriuki, IPPF's programme officer for the region, leading to serious medical risks and harmful psychological and social consequences.

This is particularly true in countries where marriage is postponed as far as possible until economic independence is reached, or where legal marriage may not even be envisaged, at least for some social groups. In these circumstances the effects of early pregnancy can be devastating educationally, social and economically. This is why attention should be focused on adolescent girls: they are the ones whose opportunities are most threatened by early pregnancy.

Early pregnancy is not, of course, found only in the developing world. The teenage pregnancy rate has been called a major public health problem in the United States. It has been estimated that over half of the 21 million adolescents aged between 15 and 19 in the United States have been sexually active and more then a million teenage girls become pregnant every year, at least two-thirds of them without planning to and most while unmarried. Thirty thousand of those pregnancies affect girls under 15 and about 430,000 teenagers have induced abortions each year.

In may countries pregnancy out of wedlock is not acceptable. It may be regarded as a sin and disgrace to the women and her whole family. Strong social pressure may lead to a forced marriage or illegal abortion and may provoke the woman to suicide or result in her murder.

As for her child, it too may suffer since the very young mother is likely to be less able to take care of it and may even be driven to killing it either actively or by neglect. Illegitimate children may face social and legal discrimination as well as economic hardship.

The psychological impact of pregnancy on a young, unmarried woman is well known. She may be disturbed by the strain of adjusting to parenthood and by her rejection, or the possibility of it, by the rest of the community. If a marriage is forced on her or if she rushes into one, it may not be a satisfactory solution since it has a higher probability of ending in failure.

The psychological and social effects of early pregnancy, on women and their children, are long lasting. In developing countries especially, pregnant adolescents, married or not, tend to leave school. For the married this is likely to be the start of a pattern of repeated childbearing. For the unmarried a return to school may be impossible because they are thought to have set a bad example to other pupils.

When the educational attainment of women is impaired in this way, it helps to perpetuate the low status of women from one generation to the next. Their opportunities for employment will be fewer and the likelihood is that they will continue to be dependent on others for their livelihood. And the cycle repeats itself in another way. The children of teenage mothers are very likely to become teenage mothers themselves, and so the deprivation continues. In addition, the children of very young mothers are likely to be less well nourished and care for than those of more mature women. This is particularly true if the family of a pregnant girl is unwilling to give economic or emotional support.

From Africa come reports of an increasing number of cases of sexually transmitted diseases. One study found that a fifth of the schoolgirls in the Yaounde area of Cameroon were suffering from gonorrhea. In most STD clinics in Britain between 40 and 50 per cent of the female patients are under the age of 20. Professor Fathalla conforms that one effect of greater sexual activity among adolescents has been a rapid increase in sexually transmitted diseases. There are some medical factors too, such as an increase in asymptomatic infections and a growing resistance to antibiotics. The availability of modern treatment may create a sense of carelessness about these diseases even though the efficacy of such treatment cannot always be guaranteed. Finally, in some areas, modern methods of contraception have replaced condoms, which offer protection against STDs.

One serious consequence of STD is the permanent impairment of the capacity to have children if gonorrhea spreads to the Fallopian tubes in the female or the vas deferens in the male. In addition, it is known that intercourse and pregnancy at a very young age are two of several factors associated with cervical cancer.

All over the world, abortion is a pressing issue. There is no doubt that the number of abortions performed each year is growing but information is sketchy because so many women are reluctant to talk about their experiences, especially in countries where the procedure is illegal. Estimates suggest that somewhere between 30 million and 55 million abortions take place each year throughout the world, and about half of them are illegal. A substantial proportion of all abortions are performed on teenagers.

These facts about the size of the adolescent fertility problem and the dangers of early pregnancy are not widely enough known. Participants recommended that the IPPF and their planned parenthood organizations should be more active in spreading the information as widely as possible, but especially to doctors, teachers, parents and administrators as well as among adolescents.

Medical hazards of early childbearing

The social and psychological risks an early pregnancy carries for the mother have been described and it it clear that they are more serious for unmarried women than married ones. When the medical risks are discussed that distinction is lost and for married adolescent women there is the likelihood that a reproductive life begun early is one that will be longer and more taxing than one which begins late. There are, in addition, sound medical reasons for delaying the first pregnancy until a woman is in her late teens.

The younger the mother the more serious the physical consequences of pregnancy are likely to be. Complications in pregnancy and childbirth or puerperium (including induced abortion) are ranked as a leading cause of death for women aged between 15 and 19 in developing countries. The ones who survive may suffer from physical ill-effects for the rest of their lives.

The age of the woman affects the outcome of the pregnacy as well as the mother's health. Pre-natal mortality rates are considerably higher with very young teenage mothers than older ones. Their babies are more likely to have a lowbirth weight, to die or to get ill than the babies of slightly older mothers.

It is important to distinguish between younger adolescents and older ones when discussing the risks of pregnacy. For women aged 18 or 19 the factor of age barely adds to the hazards of pregnancy and at any age good obstetric and antenatal care, nutrition and general health are significant factors.

Age seems to make most difference when the mother is 15 or under. For women who become pregnant before they are 15 maternal morality is 60 per cent higher than for women in general. Mothers under 15 are 3.5 times more likely to die from toxemia. Infant mortality is 2.4 times higher for babies born to mothers aged under 15 than for babies born to mothers in their early twenties.

Specifically, there are two main obstetric risks for the young, pregnant adolescent. Toxemia, which carries the risk of eclampsia and which can endanger the life of the mother and foetus; and cephalopelvic disproportion, which occurs if pregnancy takes place before the pelvis has reached its mature size, causing difficulties in labour and delivery.

One risk to the baby if its mother is a young adolescent is low birth-weight, which makes it more likely to die at birth or in infancy and can affect its physical and mental development. There is also an increased chance of the baby having neurological defects which may leave it mentally retarded for life.

These risks are important for two reasons. First, they give weight to the argument that it is better for young adolescent women to wait until they are in their late teens before starting a family. The need here is for good accessible contraceptive services to be provided and promoted so that they are widely used. Secondly, they show how important it is to encourage women to use obstetric services, where they are available, as early in the pre-natal period as possible.

HEALTH IMPLICATIONS OF ADOLESCENT PREGNANCY

Risks to the mother

The health risks to the teenage mother fall into two broad categories: first, the problems, still imperfectly understood, which flow from the fact that the teenage mother is herself still growing, and, second, the better known and more easily documented medical risks that arise with greater frequency during the course of a teenage pregnancy and delivery.

During that time a young woman will be experiencing hormonal changes which operate to control her linear growth; how these are affected by pregnancy is incompletely understood. What gives some cause for concern in this regard is the knowledge that the administration of estrogens to growing girls accelerates epidphysical maturation, and if administered in large does is believed by some to cause premature fusion. More importantly, young women who do complete a pregnancy apparently fuse their epiphyses during the nine months of gestation.

The importance of physical maturity is also appaent in

data concerning pregnancy outcomes. Evidence suggests that the body of the girl who conceives within two years of menarche (regardless of chronological age if under sixteen) is less able to produce a healthy infant. Those girls produce twice as many low birth weight infants as do mothers who are eaually young but who first conceive more than twenty-four months after menarche.

What we know about the actual course of the teenage pregnancy and delivery lends weight to the belief that pregnancy among girls fifteen years of age and under carries greater risk than does pregnancy among women in their twenties. Four problems are well-documented and paraticularly common:

- Teenagers are more likely to suffer from anemia during their pregnancies.
- Teenagers experience a higher incidence of toxemia, which in its most serious forms may result in high blood pressure, seizures, and sometimes death.
- There is a greater likelihood fo prolonged labour, which mutiplies the hazards to the mother and her child.

Risks to the infant

The difficulties that arise for the mother have a direct bearing on the risks faced by the infant, for whom they are both more obvious and frequently more severe . Whatever difficulties there may have in documenting the potential risks to the young mother, the dangers faced by their infants are unambiguous. In the United States, the babies born to very young mothers are three times as likely to die in the first year of life, and more than twice as likely to be born weighing less than 2500 grams.

The cutoff used to identify low birth weight infants is 2500 grams, and we have come to know it as one of the most accurate predictors of health status (predicting health problems in the first seven years of life). Low birth weight infants, including those born to teenage mothers, are more likely to suffer from birth-related defects such as mental retardation, deafness, cerebral palsy, seizure disorders, blindness, and other congenital anomalies. In addition, these infants start life with less iron than larger babies.

One particularly striking bit of data will help to make this point. Children born to women fifteen years of age and under have three and one-half times the number of neurologic abnormalities than children born to older women. Although these data come from the United States, a brief overview of the international literature suggests that similar risks are faced by infants born to the teenage mothers in other countries.

Repeated pregnancies

The first-born child of a teenage mother faces formidable obstacles at the start of life, but the adverse effects of teenage pregnancies multiply when those mothers have a second child before the age of twenty. Infant mortality and maternal mortality rates increase with successive births and short intervals between births.

But the more telling point is made by statistics on neonatal deaths. Those are the deaths which occur in the first twenty-eight days of life, and which reflect not so much the poverty of the family or the quality of the food and housing available to the growing infant, but the health status of the mother and the conditions immediately surrounding pregnancy and delivery. And those deaths increase dramatically among the second, third, and subsequent children born to a mother who is still in her teens.

The issue is particularly important because having a first child at a very young age increases the likelihood of additional children within a short period of time. When contraceptive programmes are not available, teenagers are most likely to have a second pregnancy. Eighteen percent will be pregnant within six months after their first delivery, nearly half will be by the end of two years, and virtually all will have been by the end of five years. the details are less important than the conclusion: very early pregnancies are almost never a one-time occurrence, and multiple pregnancies among very young mothers almost always involve substantially greater risks.

In the past, even when family planning programmes were available, as many as one-half of all very young mothers became pregnant again within three years of having their first child. This appears to have been true even when a full range of services was available to the mothers and their infants. In the United States, where young pregnancies are often frowned upon, many communities have established programmes in the hope that providing comprehensive health, education, and social services will prevent a second pregnancy. Yet even in one of the best of these- a program conducted in conjunction with the Yale University Medical School in New Haven, Connecticut- that proved to be not enough. All of the mothers in the programme received a full range of contraceptive services and information, along with other forms of assistance, but of 180 mothers studied, 79 had delivered one or more infants within the two-to-four-year period following their first pregnancy. Still others were known to be pregnant or to have had spontaneous miscarriages before the time of the study's final interview.

Here too, with all of the advantages of medical management and social services, the health risk to second and subsequent infants remained dramatically higher. In the Yale program, the health status of the infants dropped significantly with each subsequent birth. Perinatal deaths were seven times more likely among second children, and double that figure for the third child. Prematurity, or low birth weight, increased geometrically, from 11 per cent among first children to 21 per cent among second children, and 43 per cent among third children.

With such dramatic outcomes one might expect simple explanations. Perhaps if we knew more that would be true; for the present we can only speculate. The most likely explanation is that age and parity interact in ways that leave the babies of very young mothers at very high risk. What we find operating is the whole constellation of factors that make the crucial difference between a healthy, normal pregnancy and a troubled, high risk one; nutrition, physical development, hormonal maturity, and general health status, as well as more external forces like poverty and the availability of adequate medical care.

2.6 MORAL CODE OF ETHICS- THEIR ROLES AND FUNCTIONS

Objectives :

1. To understand what is meant by code of ethics or morality.

2. To be aware of the complexities and difficulties involved in deciding what is morally right or wrong.

3. To be aware of the existence of the various theories on moral behaviour.

4. To understand the concept of morality in relation to the family, peers, religion, culture, education and political system, with emphasis on the confusion and conflicts between the older and younger generation.

Time Required : 120 minutes.

Materials : Mahjong paper: cellophane/mask tape; marker pen. Information Sheets.

PROCEDURE

At the outset, the teacher should be aware that morality cannot be taught through instruction alone. The development of morality is dependent on many factors which interact in a complex manner in an individual making a moral decision. Morality is a subjective concept and its definition varies from culture to culture and from period to period. For example, what is morally right today may not be acceptable in the future. There are many instances in which the moral standards in one culture contradict with those of another.

Based on these principles, the teacher should guide the discussion sessions to:

a) create awareness of the factors which influence moral decisions, and

b) develop understanding of the internal confusion and conflicts in moral decision- making of the individual.

The purpose of this section is to create awareness of moral issues among the youth. During the discussion it is hoped that the students will undergo an experiential kind of learning, which will enable them to understand differences in opinions, as well as the importance of a "norm" or "societal code of rules" in regulating human behaviour for the common good of the society. The teacher may introduce Kholberg's Theory on the stages of moral reasoning. However, it should be pointed out that this is only a theory to explain moral development. The trainer need not spend too much time on it. An introduction of the general aspects of the theory is sufficient.

During discussions of moral issues, the teacher should not at any time impose his/her values or moral stand on the students and should maintain an open view, thus enabling the students to decide what is moral and immoral. He/she should only highlight the complexities involved in moral decisions and identify factors that contribute to the differences or similarities of moral standards of people.

Step

1. The participants are divided into small groups of five to ten. Each group elects a leader.
2. The class teacher prepares beforehand Mahjong paper and distribute it to each group.
3. Ask the participants to write down the meaning of "code of ethics" or morality. Lead the discussion to clarify the meaning.
4. Distribute Worksheet 2.7.1 and the Information Sheets pp. 64-68. Definition of Moral Stages.
5. The leader of each sub-group can ask each member to list down on Worksheet 2.6.1 items which are considered morally right or wrong. The leader should stimulate discussion on these items for about 15 minutes. The group's findings are written on Mahjong paper.
6. Distribute Worksheets for pictures 2.7.2 and 2.7.3.
7. Any or all three anecdotes in Activities 2.6.2 and 2.6.3 can be used in the group discussion, which can be based on questions suggested in the Worksheet for any anecdote selected. Time allocated for the discussion is 15 minutes. Answers are written on Mahjong paper.
8. During the plenary session, the group outputs are displayed along the wall. The teacher, assisted by the group leaders, summarizes major aspects of the discussion on moral issues.

9. Distribute the Information Sheets on Kholberg's stages of Moral Reasoning and Levels of Awareness and Consequences.

10. The teacher runs through the Information Sheets points out how the discussions fall into various levels of moral reasoning.

11. The teacher, assisted by the group leaders, identify the roles of individuals in the family and society and explains potential conflicts between the older and younger generations. The students try to summarize and form conclusions.

INFORMATION SHEET

Kholberg's Stages of Moral Reasoning

1. Pre-conventional Level

At this level, the child is responsive to cultural rules and labels of good and bad, right or wrong, but interprets these labels in terms of either the physical or the hedonistic consequences of action (punishment, reward, exchange of favours or in terms of the physical power of those who enunciate the rules and labels). The level is divided into the following two stages:

Stage 1 *The punishment and obedience orientation.* The physical consequences of action to determine its goodness or badness regardless of the human meaning or value of these consequences. Avoidance of punishment and unquestioning deferencc to power are valued in their own right, not in terms of respect for an underlying moral order supported by punishment and authority (the later being Stage 4).

Stage 2 *The instrumental relativist orientation.* Right action consists of that which instrumentally satisfies one's own needs and occasionally the needs of others. Human relations are viewed in terms like those of the market place. Elements of fairness, or reciprocity and equal sharing are present, but they are always interpreted in a physical pragmatic way. Reciprocity is a matter of "you scratch my back and I'll scratch yours, "not of loyalty, gratitude or justice.

II. Conventional level

At this level, maintaining the expectations of the individual's family, group or nation is perceived as valuable in its own right, regardless of immediate and obvious consequences. The attitude is not only one of *conformity* to personal expectations and social order, but of loyalty to it, of actively *maintaining*, supporting, and justifying the order and of identifying with the persons or group involved in it. At this level, these are the following two stages:

Stage 3 *The interpersonal concordance or "good boy-nice girl" orientation.* Good behaviour is that which pleases or helps and is approved. There is much conformity to stereotypical images of what is majority or "natural" behaviour. Behaviour is frequently judged by intention- "he means well" becomes important for the first time. One earns approval by being "nice".

Stage 4 *The "law and order" orientation.* There is orientation toward authority, fixed rules, and the maintenance of the social order. Right behaviour consists of doing one's duty. Showing respect for authority and maintaining the given social order for its own sake.

III. Post-conventional, autonomous, or principled level

At this level, there is a clear effort to define moral values and principles which have validity and application apart from the authority of the groups or persons holding these principles and apart from the individual's own identification with these groups. This level again has two stages:

Stage 5 *The social contract legalistic orientation.* Generally with utilitarian overtones. Right action tends to be defined in terms of general individual rights and in terms of standards which have been critically examined and agreed upon by the whole society. There is a clear awareness of the relativism of personal values and opinions and a corresponding emphasis upon procedural rules for reaching consensus. Aside from what is constitutionally and democratically agreed upon, the right is a matter of personal "values" and "opinion". The result is an emphasis upon the "legal point of view", but with an emphasis upon the possibility of changing law in terms of rational considerations of social utility, (rather than freezing it in terms of Stage 4 "law and order"). Outside the legal realm, free agreement, and contract is the binding element of obligation. This is the "official" morality of the American government and Constitution.

Stage 6 *The universal ethical principle orientation.* Right is defined by the decision of conscience in accord with self-chosen ethical, principles appealing to logical comprehensiveness, universality, and consistancy. These principles are abstract and ethical, (the Golden Rule, the categorical imperative) they are not concrete moral rules like the Ten Commandments. At heart, these are universal principles of *justice* of the *reciprocity* and *equality* of the human rights and of respect for the dignity of human beings as *individual persons.*

SIX STAGES IN CONCEPTION OF THE MORAL WORTH OF HUMAN LIFE

The following categorizes the answers given to the questions and the case stories reprinted in Suggested Activities 2.7.2, according to L. Kholberg's six stages of moral reasoning.

Stage 1 No differentiation between moral value of life and its physical or social-status value.

Tomy, age ten (why should the druggist give the drug to the dying woman when her husband couldn't pay for it?): "If someone important is in a plane and is allergic and the stewardess won't give him medicine because she's only got enough for one and she's got a sick one, a friend, they'd probably put the stewardess in a lady's jail because she didn't help the important one".

(Is it better to save the life of one important person or a lot of unimportant people?): "All the people that aren't important because one man just has one house, maybe a lot of furniture, but a whole bunch of people have an awful lot of furniture and some of these poor people might have an awful lot of money and it doesn't look it."

Stage 2 The value of a human life is seen as instrumental to the satisfaction of the needs of its possessor or of other persons. Decision to save life is relative to, or to be made by, its possessor. (Differentiation of physical and interest value of life, differentiation of its value to self and to other.)

Tomy, age thirteen (Should the doctor" mercy kill" a fatally ill woman requesting death because of her pain?): "Maybe it would be good to put her out of her pain, she'd be better off that way. But the husband wouldn't want it, it's not like an animal. If a pet dies you can get along without it-it isn't something you really need. Well, you can get a new wife, but it's not really the same."

Jim, age thirteen (same question): "If she requests it, it's really up to her. She is in such terrible pain, just the same as people are always putting animals out of their pain."

Stage 3 The value of human life is based on the empathy and affection of family members and others toward its possessor. (The value of human life, as based on social sharing, community and love, is differentiated from the instrumental and hedonistic value of life applicable also to animals.

Tomy, age sixteen (same question): "It might be best for her, but her husband -it's a human life-not like an animal, it just doesn't have the same relationship that a human being does to a family. You can become attached to dog, but nothing like a human you know".

Stage 4 Life is conceived as sacred in terms of its place in a categorical moral or religious order of rights and duties. (The value of human life, as a categorical member of a moral order, is differentiated from its value to specific other people in the family, etc. Value of life is still partly dependent upon serving the group, the state, God, however.)

Jim, age sixteen (same question): "I don't know. In one way, it's murder, it's not a right or privilege of man to decide who shall live and who should die. God put life into everybody on earth and you're taking away something from that person that came directly from God, and you're destroying something that is very sacred, it's in a way part of God and it's almost destroying a part of God when you kill a person. There's something of God in everyone".

Stage 5 Life is valued both in terms of its relation to community welfare and in terms of being a universal human right. (Obligation to respect the basic right to life is differentiated from generalized respect for the sociomoral order. The general value of the independent human life is a primary autonomous value not independent upon other values).

Jim, age twenty (same question): "Given the ethics of the doctor who has taken on responsibility to save human life-from that point of view he probably shouldn't but there is another side, there are more and more people in the medical profession who are thinking it is a hardship on everyone, the person, the family, when you know they are going to die. When a person is kept alive by an artificial lung or kidney it's more like being a vegetable than being a human who is alive. If it's her wone choice I think there are certain rights and privileges that go along with being a hman being. I am a human being and have certain desires for life and I think everybody else does too. You have a world of which you are the center, and everybody else does too and in that sense we're all equal."

Stge 6 Belief in sacredness of human life as representing a univrsal human value of respect for the individual.

(The moral value of a human being, as an object of moral principle, if differentiated from a formal recognition of its rights.)

Jim, age twenty-four (Should the husband steal the drug to save his wife? How about for someone he just know?): "Yes. A human life takes precedence over any other moral or legal value, whoever it is. A human life has inherent value whether or not it is valued by a particular individual."

(Why is that?): "The inherent worth of the individual human being is the central value in a set of values where the principles of justice and love are normative for all human relationships."

LEVELS OF AWARENESS OF CONSEQUENCES

The following sequence of levels of awareness of consequences is an interpretation of the research reported by Lawrence Kohlberg and his colleagues (1975).

Unaware of consequences (level 0)

Very young children are largely unaware of the consequences of their acts. Impulsiveness is the mode.

"I just did it because I wanted to".

Punishment (Level 1)

Soon enough, punishment comes into awareness. Children become aware that they might be punished for their acts. Especially if they feel vulnerable, they will tend to be obedient and defer to power once they reach this level of awareness.

"I don't want to get into trouble."

Self-interest (Level 2)

Next comes an awareness of our own interest, or what meets personal needs, of what gives gratification. Immediate gratification is often sought first at this stage. Awareness of the needs of other is also growing, but others are mostly used to trade off pleasures; the focus remains on self interests.

"I need others to take care of me".

"I helped you last time. This time you should help me".

Approval from others (Level 3)

There next develops a clear awareness that others observe us and judge us. And with it comes an interest in winning the approval of others. A person now can find satisfaction in being seen as a "good guy" or a "good gal". We can now also appreciate more of others' internal states and thus consider the consequences an act might have on another's feelings as well as on our own.

"I hope I was a good boy today".

"Sally was trying to help us even though she messed up the game".

Stability and structure (Level 4)

The next new element added seems to be an awareness of social structures and the importance of those structures in controlling behaviours. People who have reached this level make reference to specific rules and sometimes place great value on law and order. They are often ready to punish severely those who violate stability. Their interest is in keeping things steady rather than in progress. People at this level can appreciate the importance of loyalty to a group.

"Everyone should believe in the Ten Commandments".

Individuality (Level 5)

Human variability seems to be the next element to be appreciated. We begin to appreciate people different from ourselves. There is a willingness to bend laws to allow individual needs. There is also a willingness to change individual laws to meet the needs of the group better. Freedom becomes highly regarded. This stage develops with a flexibility and an openness to change not seen at earlier stages. There is more tolerance for ambiguity and uncertainty. There also develops a respect for the process by which issues are resolved. Due process and rational deliberation come to be seen as more important than existing laws and rules.

"We should all cooperate and decide what's best."

"There are exceptions to every rule."

Complex whole with an emphasis on justice (Level 6)

We next see developed an appreciation and respect for interdependence. A person's view reaches for comprehension of all life. Any individual's rights are seen as dependent on the integrity of the complex whole. people who reach this level are able to feel the nobility of personal sacrifice performed for the good of the whole. They may feel proud to defy a law for a greater good. Often they can verbalize personal principles of life. No longer is law or even collective decision making seen as paramount; personal integrity and conscience are viewed as even more fundamental.

"I try to live by treating others the way I would want others to treat me if our positions were reversed".

SUGGESTED ACTIVITY 2.6.1

Worksheet 2.1: What is right and what is wrong?

Write five morally right and five morally wrong statements concerning marriage, parents, and sex.

		Morally right statements	*Morally wrong statements*
Marriage	1)	____________	____________
	2)	____________	____________
	3)	____________	____________
	4)	____________	____________
	5)	____________	____________
Parents	1)	____________	____________
	2)	____________	____________
	3)	____________	____________
	4)	____________	____________
	5)	____________	____________
Sex	1)	____________	____________
	2)	____________	____________
	3)	____________	____________
	4)	____________	____________
	5)	____________	____________

SUGGESTED ACTIVITY 2.6.2

Anecdotes for group discussion

1. Joe and his father

Joe is a fourteen yearold boy who wanted to go to camp very much. His father promised him he could go if he saved up the money for it himself. So Joe worked hard at his paper route and saved up the $ 40 it cost to go to camp and a little more besides. But just before camp was going to start, his father changed his mind. Some of his friends decided to go on a special fishing trip, and Joe's father was short of the money it would cost. So he told Joe to give him the money he had saved from the paper route. Joe didn't want to give up going to camp so he thought of refusing to give his father the money.

Suggestion for discussion

1. Should Joe give his money to his father?
2. Is it proper for Joe's father to ask for the money?

2. Rahman

A woman was near death from a special kind of cancer. There was one drug that the doctors thought might save her. It was a form of radium that a druggist in the same town had recently discovered. The drug was expensive to make, but the druggist was charging ten times what the drug cost him to make. He paid $200 for the radium and charged $2,000 for a small dose of the drug. The sick woman's husband, Rahman went to everyone he knew to borrow the money, but he could only get together about $ 1,000 which is half of what it cost. He told the druggist that his wife was dying, and asked him to sell it cheaper or let him pay later. But the druggist said, 'No.1 discovered the drug and I'm going to make money from it.' So Rahman got desperate and broke into the man's store to steal the drug for his wife.

Suggestions for discussion

1. In Rahman's story, who is at fault, Rahman or druggist?
2. Is it all right for a person to steal?

3. Doctor

The doctor finally got some of the radium drug for Rahman's wife. But it didn't work and there was no other treatment known to medicine which would save her. So the doctor knew that she had about six months to live. She was in terrible pain, but she was so weak that a good dose of a pain-killer like ether or morphine would make her die sooner. She was delirious and almost crazy with pain, and in her calm periods she would ask the doctor to give her enough ether to kill her. She said she couldn't stand the pain and she was going to die in a few months anyway.

Suggestions for Discussion

1. Should the Doctor give ether to Rahman's wife?
2. Does the doctor have the right to give her ether?

SUGGESTED ACTIVITY 2.6.3

To Help or Not to Help

A teacher asks you if you want to help some other students. Decide if you do want to help them. Put a check mark by the one thought that would be most like yours. Which of the following sounds most like you?

__________ Will I get punished if I don't do it?

__________ What's in it for me? Will I get help when I need it?

__________ If I help them, will the other students end up liking me more?

__________ Is there a rule about helping in situations like this one?

__________ What is best for all of us, all things considered?

__________ As I think about this situation and the kind of person I want to be, what is the best thing for me to do?

MODULE 3

SEX ROLES

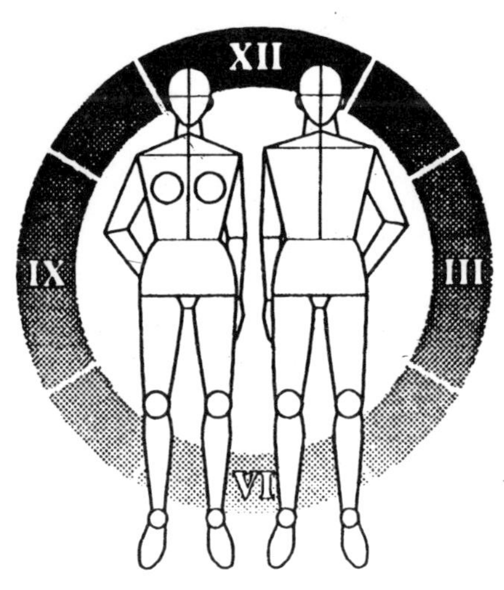

3

SEX ROLES

This is the third of a serious of four modules that comprises a package entitled Adolescence Education. This module on sex roles deals with role expectations, male and female roles and stereotyping. This particular module consists of the following lessons and their corresponding objectives:

Topics	Objectives
Lesson 3.1 Role Expectations	1) To examine and understand attitudes towards sex, men, women and youth. 2) To identify and discuss the role expectations of men, women, and youth, in the family and society. 3) To be aware of child rearing practices in the family and in society as they affect sex role development.
Lesson 3.2 Male and Female Roles	1) To define the meaning of sex roles. 2) To describe how different cultures look at sex roles. 3) To identify the different roles of men and women. 4) To identify the various stereotypes developed for men and women.
Lesson 3.3 Being Masculine/ Feminine	To increase the student's awareness of the stereotyped sex roles and to encourage them to notice how they compare

	themselves to stereotypes.
Lesson 3.4 Stereotype Voting	1) To help students develop more under standing about masculinity and femininity. 2) To compare ideas and explore sex role stereotyping.

Each lesson is provided with a set of objectives and indicates the time required for teaching, the materials to be used and the set of procedures to be followed in carrying out the teaching. Information sheets to help teachers in expanding the subject, reference materials and activities/exercises for students are also provided.

3.1 ROLE EXPECTATIONS

Objectives :

1. To examine and understand attitudes towards sex, men; women, and youth.
2. To identify and discuss the role expectations of men, women and youth, in the family and society.
3. To be aware of child rearing practices in the family and in society as they affect sex role development.

Time Required : 90 minutes

Materials : White board/blackboard; marker pen and duster/ chalk; masking tape/cellophane tape; synopsis of a film; blank writing paper. Information Sheet.

SYNOPSIS OF THE FILM : SEX ROLE DEVELOPMENT

INTRODUCTION

The film "Sex-Role Development" examines the influence played by sex roles and stereotypes on almost every facet of life. The film also discusses such questions as; "Are there innate reasons for different male and female standards? Is there truth in the stereotypes of 'maleness' and femaleness?' If so what are they?" "How can sex-role stereotypes be eradicated from a society that strictly subscribes to such stereotypes?" " Is it possible to select the best male and female roles and combine them, so as to enable a person to respond in the most effective manner possible to any situation?" " Can the future generation profit from attempts to bring them up in non-sexist ways?" " "Will they demand a return to traditional sex roles, or will they perhaps create different roles?" These questions, of course, have no definitive answers. The purpose of the film is to present some of many potential answers, in an effort to be effective stimulus for class discussion and exploration.

The film opens with some examples of common sex-role stereotypes and then illustrates various ways of teaching these stereotype sex roles to children, including the use of books, television, toys, as well as through peer behaviour and the direct and indirect communication of adult expectations. In an interview sequence, Dr. Peter Bentler, a psychologist from UCLA, discusses the consequences of sex-role stereotyping. For instance, both men and women rate the quality of a piece of work that is attributed to a woman as being poorer, compared with the same work that is attributed to a man. Dr. Bentler further discusses one of the more important ideas stemming from sex-role research, that is, the concept of androgyny, with the idea that the best of the male and female sex roles can be combined, so that people can behave flexibly and effectively in any given situation. For instance, a woman can have the flexibility to behave aggnessively or a man can behave emotionally without fear of being labeled "sissy". The remainder of the film is devoted to two examples in which non-traditional sex-role philosophy pervades the socialization of particular children.

The viewers are introduced to a family with a three-year old son. The family members go about their daily activities and the parents discuss their ideas about sex roles. They feel strongly against making distinctions between "boy" and "girl" behaviour and believe that treating boys and girls equally is a goal-oriented philosophy, in which parents and others socializing agents prepare children for their adult life from the time of their birth. The parents believe that stereotyping robs the children of a wide variety of life experiences that can enrich the process of growing up.

The setting of the film moves to a nursery school that is

dedicated to providing a non-stereotyped environment for children during these early years when sex-role attitudes are being formed. The school provides similar experiences for all children, with the hope of eliminating some of the artificial boy-girl differences created by society. The aim is not to make boys and girls the same, but rather to assist the development of each child as an individual and to help each attain his or her own unique level of growth. The teachers actively teach the children to accept one another as individuals, and consciously try to bridge the gap between the non-stereotyped environment of the school and that of the larger society where sexual stereotypes abound.

The film closes with a discussion of thought-provoking questions: "What will be the reaction of future generations to our attempts at raising children in non-sexist ways?" "Will they be happier, more fulfilled individuals, or will they reject our attempts and again demand a differentiation in sex roles?"

PROCEDURE

Step 1 Distribute writing sheets.

Step 2 Read the synopsis of the film, "Sex Role Development" and lead a discussion on the following:

DISCUSSION QUESTIONS

1. Discuss a child's typical socializing experiences which help him or her inculcate the sex roles that will regulate much of his or her later life.

2. Discuss specific ways by which sex-role stereotypes influence personal perceptions, attitudes and expectations, as well as those we have of others. What sort of behaviour is expected of boys and of girls?

3. Recall the differences in the ways by which sons and daughters in your family were brought up. Did the boys seem to have an advantage over the girls? If so, how do you feel about this?

4. What is the role of the media in creating and perpetuating sex-role stereotypes?

5. In what ways (if any) would you like to see sex roles change? Why?

6. If you were a parent today, how would you handle the sex-role development of your child or children?

7. How can parents, teachers, and other socializing agents help children to reconcile the differences between a non-sexist environment and an environment which reinforces sexual stereotypes?

8. What steps can the society take to change traditional sex roles and to reduce current sex-role stereotypes?

9. How will future generations respond to contemporary ideas concerning raising children in non-sexist ways? Explain.

INFORMATION SHEET

Role Expectations

Studies investigating sex-role stereotype indicate that generally, men and women hold similar stereotypes of the characteristics typical of males and females: males are logical, dominant, independent, unemotional and aggressive; women are sensitive, emotional, nurturant, use intuition, and are somewhat dependent and submissive. Even more significant are findings that indicates that adult men and women see themselves as fitting these stereotypes and that health care workers tend to label the psychologically healthy person as one who conforms to these stereotypes.

It is unlikely that such personality characteristics are completely innate because in some cultures, the women are aggressive and dominant and the men are the ones who are emotional and sensitive. If there are inherent predispositions that are different for each sex it appears that the particular culture accentuates some and masks others. In many societies, boys and girls are treated differently from the time they are born. Girls receive more affection and physical contact, are talked to more protected more, and have more restrictions placed on them: boys enjoy more independence and more achievement demands. At age two or two and one-half, children can identify themselves as a boy or girl and they openly seek and receive information about what being a boy or girl means. A boy will grow up to be like daddy. Does he want to be a fireman, doctor, astronaut, or perhaps the president of the country? A girl will grow up like mommy, to have children and to maybe become a nurse, executive secretary or teacher as well. Boys are told not to be sissies and girls not to be tomboys. Boys are discouraged from showing their emotions and girls from being aggressive. They are even given different toys.

In public schools sex roles are further developed and reinforced. Girls are directed to the doll corner and they jump ropes and while boys are directed to the blocks and balls. Primary readers portray Mom taking care of the house and Dad going off to the office. Little girls are portrayed as observers and perpetually afraid and little boys as brave, active problem solvers. Girls are expected to be good at spelling and have pretty handwriting and boys are expected to be good at math and be interested in mechanical endeavours.

One adolescence is reached, the motivation to be feminine or masculine is increased as a result of pressures to conform to peer group expectations. As adulthood approaches and life's options become more obvious, feminity and masculinity also become more narrowly defined. If is not until this time that girls' academic performance, previously superior to boys', tend to drop, sometimes drastically. It is "unfeminine" to be intellectually superior to boys and to compete with them. The decline in academic performance may also be due to the poor analytic ability typical of girls, which tends to become more important in the upper grades. Research findings suggest that early independence training, usually stressed more for boys, might be the key to the development of analytic thinking. For instance, studies have found relationships between parental encouragement of independence and self-assertion and their children's analytic ability and increasing IQ. Furthermore, boys who are over protected tend to develop similarly to girls intellectually, whereas girls who excel in analytic abilities tend to be those who reject identification with traditional feminine roles. Rejection of society's expectations and role definitions is often done at the cost of conflict, tension and anxiety.. However, accepting traditional sex roles also has its toll on the individual.

Although there is a shortage of studies of the psychological consequences of sex-role demand on men, such consequences are obviously heavy. Men are locked into the role of being the strong, dependable, breadwinner and restricted in their expression of emotion—a dictate to deny part of themselves and one that too often results in the denial of open and intimate relationships as well. Most men do not have the option of staying in the home and watching their children grow while their wives assume the role of family supporter. Although the couple might be happier with this division of labour, it is a rare man, particu-larly a middle-class one, who can comfortably flaunt the demands of society. Pressure to achieve money and status is responsible for a high degree of tension, stress and anxiety and perhaps contributes to the high rate of heart attacks among middle-aged men.

Research on the psychological consequences of sex-roles for women is more abundant. Women occupy an inferior social status and a subordinate social role. Traditional unquestioning acceptance of such a position has had devastating consequences for them. Research indicates that girls' self-esteem and self-opinions become progressively poorer with age. Other studies have found that women are prejudiced against women (in a recent study in which college students were asked which sex they would prefer if they could have only one child. 91 per cent of the men and 66 per cent of the women said they would prefer a male), value "Male characteristics" more then "female" ones, believe men are more suited for high status positions and minimize accomplishments if they are attributed to women. It appears that even women who are oriented toward achievement tend to have a concomitant fear of actually succeeding—at least in intellectual or academic pursuits. Sandra and Daryl Ben have described the consequences of sex roles on women very well: "When a baby boy is born, it is difficult to predict what he will be doing twenty-five years later. We cannot say whether he will be an artist or a doctor or a college professor because he will be permitted to develop and fulfill his own unique potential, particularly if he is white and middle class. But if the new born child is a girl, we can usually predict with confidence how she will be spending her time twenty-five years later. Her individuality doesn't have to be considered; it is irrelevant."

3.2 MALE AND FEMALE ROLES

Objectives :

1. To define the meaning of sex roles.
2. To describe how different cultures look at sex roles
3. To identify the different roles of men and women.
4. To identify the various stereotypes developed for men and women

Time Required 180 minutes

Materials :Magazines, scissors, glue, stories Information sheets

PROCEDURE

1. lecture on how various cultures differentiate the roles of men and women, based on the Information Sheet, pp. 23-24.
2. Explain the consensus of many experts on the idea that the pressure, anxiety and confusion surrounding male and female roles are core issues in most concerns related to sexuality. Male pressure to perform, female pressure to have children, male pressure to internalize feelings, female pressure to be sexy but non-sexual, and so on are factors which contribute to the high rates of unwanted pregnancy, abortion, divorce, and sexual dissatisfaction.
3. Conduct lectures based on recent studies and cross cultural comparisons on the concept of roles and stereotypes, differentiating male/female form masculine/feminine. During the discussion, the class can examine how male and female roles are formed, and more importantly, how these roles affect the lives of men and women. Have the students cite examples from their own family and school situations. Encourage them to think about how male and female roles can influence dating and sexual patterns. As a teacher, keep in mind that the adolescent years are formative years. Young people are in the midst of defining their own sexual identity, that is, what it means for them to be either male or female, and there is considerable peer

pressure to conform to expected patterns of behaviour. By discussing these issues, students will better understand the fact that they can determine their "role" in life by themselves.

4. After the lecture, have the students carry our Activity 3.2.1;3.2.2;3.2.3;3.2.4;3.2.5;3.2.6;3.2.7;3.2.8;3.2.9;3.2.10; 3.2.11;3.2.12;3.2.13.

INFORMATION SHEET

Male and Female Roles

1. Introduction

A. Sex Roles are sets of behaviour which our society determines to be appropriate for males and females.

B. Gender refers to actual biological sex, either male or female.

C. Each culture determines its own appropriate sex roles. What is accepted in one society in terms of masculine and feminine behaviour is not necessarily accepted in another.

II. **In some cultures, some behaviours that we consider to be masculine are considered to be feminine, and vice versa. In other cultures, little distinction is made between the sexes. For examples:**

A. The Hopi Indians of North Central Arizona are a matriarchal society.

1. Names and blood lines are traced through the mother. A family member is anyone related to the mother.

2. The people are divided into clans. Each person belongs to her/his mother's clan, and all members trace their lineage back to a common mother.

3. Fathers are respected and loved. They know their own children, but they spend more time with their sisters' children than with their own.

4. Husbands and wives have specific duties and separate clan obligations, so they are free to come and go as they please. Women take care of household chores and child rearing while men work in the fields.

5. In Hopi society, children are obedient and non-competitive; they rarely quarrel, there is no vandalism and children are never punished physically.

6. "Hopi" means "people of peace". They have fought few wars and then only in defense.

7. The Hopi society desires girl babies.

B. In contrast, the Mundugumore of New Guinea are a very hostile and aggressive society of head hunters.

1. Individuals trace their kinship through parents of the opposite sex.

2. Boys are raised by their mothers and girls are raised by their fathers. Both sexes are raised in exactly the same way to become independent, aggressive and fierce.

3. Children are turned against their same sex parents and are actively disliked and unwanted. Pregnancy and nursing are disliked and avoided if possible. Infanticide is practiced.

C. The Arapesh are a mountain people also of New Guinea. In this society there are few difference in sex roles for men and women.

1. Both men and women are expected to nurture all living things.

2. Fathers participate in child rearing, and children of both sexes take care of smaller children.

3. Aggressive behaviour is disapproved of, particularly those who arouse aggression in others.

4. Parents treat boys and girls equally, and they are happy to have babies of either sex.

D. The people of Bali, an Indonesian culture, appear physically to be the opposite of western ideas of what men and women should look like.

1. The men are "effeminate" by Western standards, their arms and legs are almost free from heavy muscles. They also have slightly enlarged breasts.
2. Whenever there is any heavy work, 50 to 100 men gather to do what a few men in some society could accomplish.
3. They can work long hours at a slow pace and never seem to tire; they also sing and play all hours of the day and night.
4. The women are very boyish-looking, with slim hips and small high breasts.

III. **Historically, in our culture the concept of masculinity and femininity are categorically differentiated. Men were considered "masculine" and women were "feminine". Today, we recognize that both men and women have some of the personality traits that had been considered as belonging exclusively to the opposite sex.**

A. We can think of "masculinity" "and feminity" as opposite ends of a continuum.

Absolutely masculine-Most men-Most women-Absolutely feminine

B. Most men are not "super-masculine" and most women are not "ultrafemine." Most men do have many typically "masculine" personality traits as well as a few typically "feminine" personality traits; likewise, most women have predominantly "feminine" personality traits, along with some typically "masculine" traits.

C. Any current discussion of masculinity and feminity in our society should acknowledge that male and female roles are in a state of transition. The distinctions between masculine and feminine behaviour are not as clear a pronounced as they were for most of us a decade ago.

D. Any current discussion of male and female roles should also recognize that this is a value-laden topic area. while many people feel that the evaluation and change of traditional male and female roles is good, an equally significant group of people feel that the traditional male and female roles were better and therefore highly desirable, and essential.

IV. **We know that children learn male and female roles by age two or three, and our culture has presumed that one is better off conforming to conventional sex role expectations. A number of academic studies, however, question the desirability of these traditional male and female role expectations**

A Mussen, a child psychologist at the University of California at Berkeley, studied masculinity in the late 1940's. The subject, 17 to 18-year-old boys, were rated on a high-low masculinity scale and given the California Adjustment Inventory (a personality test). Twenty years later the follow up interviews revealed these results about the men, then age 37-38:

1. The group that had been rated as highly masculine when retested 20 years later:

a. They were less self-accepting and less dominant.

b. They had a great need to humble and degrade themselves.

c. They were rated as less sociable, less self-assured, less likely to be leaders and less introspective.

2. The group that received low-masculinity rate during adolescence was rated as warm, bright, emotionally stable, sensitive and sophisticated when retested 20 years later.

B. Studies of degrees of femininity in adolescent

girls have indicated that "highly feminine" girls are often described as very dependent, shy, soft spoken, yielding, child-like and gullible-all of which are associated with high anxiety and low social acceptance.

C. Another study has shown that boys and girls who conform to rigid traditional sex role stereotypes score lower on tests of intelligence and creativity. According to Sandra Bem, a psychologist at Stanford University, people who conform to rigid male and female roles tend to limit their life experiences and, therefore, don't score as well as those who can, and do, allow themselves to experience more.

V. **Many studies have been done on sex differences and all of these studies have revealed a minimal amount of differences. We still know very little about genetic sex differences.**

A. What we do know is that males are more aggressive physically and verbally, but *only* after age two-and-a-half. Before that age, there is no *difference* between the sexes.

B. We also know that in general girls have greater verbal ability than boys from about age 11 on.

C. There are some common myths about sex differences which have not been proved:

1 Girls are more "social" than boys.

2 Girls are more suggestible than boys.

3. Girls have lower self-esteem than boys.

4. Girls lack motivation to achieve.

5. Girls are better at rote learning.

6. Boys are more "analytic" than girls.

VI. Feminism

A. The "Women's Liberation movement" appeared in the United States in the early 1960's. *The Feminine Mystique*, the classic book by Betty Friedan, illustrated the wide-spread dissatisfaction among may women about their lives and is seen as influential in stimulating examination of male and female roles.

B. Many important ideas have come from the women's movement and are reflected in significant changes in many social institutions: art, music, literature, dating customs, marriage, fashion, employment policies, etc.

C. As women have examined male and female role stereotypes and their effects, so have men evaluated traditional definitions of masculinity, resulting in the integration of many of the traditionally feminine personality traits and activities into men's.

D. Clearly, our social institutions related to male and female roles and the family are in a state of great transition as both men and women seek balance in their lives.

SUGGESTED ACTIVITY 3.2.1

Discussion questions

1. What are the differences between men and women? Which of these differences are biological? Which are cultural?
2. How differently are girls raised from boys?
3. Describe the way your family treats its male and female members. Who washes dishes? Who usually drives the car on long trips? Who gets to stay out later? Who mows the lawn?
4. How do schools treat girls and boys differently at school?
5. Are there jobs which you consider to be only for men, or only for women?
6. What would you do if you find your four-year-old daugh-

ter playing with a fire engine? Wear overalls to school?

7. What would you say/do if your four-year-old son wanted to wear a dress? What if he wanted a doll for his birthday?

8. What do you think of the women's movement?

9. Who has it better in our society- men or women?

SUGGESTED ACTIVITY 3.2.2

Incomplete Sentences

Direction: Complete the following phrases into sentences:

1. Being a woman/man makes me feel...
2. If I were the opposite sex, my life will be different because..
3. In 10 years, I will probably spend most of my time...
4. In this society, males..
5. In this society, females...
6. Having to support a family is.../
7. Growing up female is..
8. Growing up male is...
9. The one thing that I would like to change about being a boy or a girl is...
10. Boys who wear earrings are...
11. Girls who ask boys out are...
12. Boys who cry are...
13. Boys who like to cook are...
14. Girls who are athletic are..

SUGGESTED ACTIVITY 3.2.3

Continuums/Values voting

Direction: Write agree or disagree after each of the following statements:

1. A woman´s place is in the home.
2. It´s all right for a girl to play on a male team of she's a good athlete.
3. Men should make the important decisions because men think before acting, while women act based on their emotions.
4. Husbands and wives should share equally in housework and child care.
5. Males and females are created differently and are meant to act in very different ways.
6. It's all right for a man to cry.
7. Alimony should be abolished.
8. Women are instinctively maternal and nurturing.
9. Girls should be free to ask boys for a date.
10. Most women do not want to be independent, but want a man to take care of them.
11. Women have the advantages in our society because they have protection, leisure, and freedom from the pressure to achieve.
12. It is up to the man to initiate sexual activities, but is up to the women to say yes or no.
13. Men have a stronger sex drive than women.
14. Men can have sex and enjoy it for its pleasure, but women need some kind of emotional involvement to enjoy sex.
15. Girls should pay for themselves on dates.

SUGGESTED ACTIVITY 3.2.4

Uncle Ansar's Advice Column

Dear Uncle Ansar:

I hope you don't laugh at me, too. We had a special day week called "Career Futures Day" Where everybody had to talk about the kind of career they would like to have. I've always wanted to be a dancer, modern or ballet: but in my presentation I said that I wanted to be a lawyer, because I did not want to be called a sissy. Recently, I found out that the physical Education (PE) Department is going to offer a modern dance class next semester. I'd really like to take it, but I don't want to be the only guy in the class. When I talked to my PE coach about it, he just laughed and told me to play basketball instead since I stand 6'4". What should I do?

Tall and Frustrated

SUGGESTED ACTIVITY 3.2.5

Masculine/Feminine

Define the word "stereotype". On the blackboard draw two columns- one with the heading " masculine": the other, "feminine." Ask the class to brainstorm and to list all the stereotyped characteristics they associate with either sex. What are the classic definitions of a "real man"? What are the classic definitions of a "real lady"? The class can carry out this activity together or in male/female groups. Discuss the results and synthesize the ideas of the students.

SUGGESTED ACTIVITY 3.2.6

Collage of sex stereotypes

Have each student bring a few magazine to class-family, men's, women's or children's magazines. Form small same-sex groups and give each group magazines, scissors, glue, etc. Have the male group make a collage depicting the "Woman," by cutting pictures from the magazines. Ask them to list the characteristics most commonly associated with women. Have the female group to do a similar collage and list, focussed on the "Man".

Depending on the size of the class, display the collages and have the girls review the boy's work; and vice-versa. If the class too large,have a female group join with a male group to discuss each other's work.

SUGGESTED ACTIVITY 3.2.7

Quickie

On the blackboard, draw a circle and a square of equal size.

Ask the class which one is male and which is female. Explain. Draw straight lines and squiggly lines, letters of the alphabet, numbers, almost any abstract design, including

Discuss how the students decide which drawing represents what, and what that appears to indicate.

SUGGESTED ACTIVITY 3.2.8

Famous people

Have the class list 10 famous people.
Have the class list 10 famous people from your country.
Have the class list 10 famous women from your country.

Discuss the results.

This exercise is best carried out right before the lesson on male and female roles in presented. The first two lists will take longer to complete and will probably be heavily weighted with movie/TV stars. Discuss what that implies.

Variation

Ask the class to list 10 famous politicians or 10 famous scientists. You can also ask the class to list 10 famous male movi /TV stars and 10 famous female movie/TV stars. Then discuss what qualities make a woman a star as opposed to the qualities required of a man.

SUGGESTED ACTIVITY 3.2.9

The surgeon's Dilemma

This exercise series is a fast way of getting the students to look at their own assumptions about male and female roles.

The procedure is very simple. Without explaining your purpose, distribute copies of the story below. Tell the students they have five minutes to read the story and solve the problem. They should not share their solution with anyone else.

Here's the story:

A father and his son are driving to a baseball game. On the freeway, they meet a car accident. The father is killed and the boy is brought to the hospital in an ambulance. They immediately wheel him into the operating room. The surgeon looks at the boy and becomes quite upset. "I can't operate on this child! He's my son!"

How is that possible? The solution: The surgeon is the boy's mother. An alternative version would have a mother and child in the accident, with the mother being killed. The nurse in the emergency room would be the child's father.

SUGGESTED ACTIVITY 3.2.10

Male And Female Roles and Language

The purpose of this exercise is to assist students in recognizing the role which language plays in strengthening sexual stereotypes through connotation and denotations of meaning.

PROCEDURE :

1. Ask the student to go over the different word pairs. How are the words used?

Mr. ____________________ Mrs.

Lord ____________________ Lady

King ____________________ Queen

Prince ____________________ Princess

Wizard ____________________ Witch

Bachelor ____________________ Old Maid

Master ____________________ Mistress

God ____________________ Mother Nature

landlord________________ Landlady

Patron ________________ Matron

Sir____________________ Madam

2. Ask the students to explain and discuss the different implications and connotations of each word, depending on whether it is the male or female indicator. How does wizard differ from witch? Master from mistress? Mr. from Mrs..?

3. Discuss whether language strengthens sexual stereotypes? (use of male pronouns, such as chairman, mankind, etc.) Should society attempt to change a language that reinforces sexual stereotypes?

SUGGESTED ACTIVITY 3.2.11

Because I am... If I were...

This activity will help the student explore and clarify his/her concepts of male and female roles. It is particularly helpful in exploring how rigid male and female roles can limit an individual's self-expression. Students also gain a greater understanding of the concerns of the members of the opposite sex.

PROCEDURE:

1. Divide the students into two groups: male and female.
2. Give each group two large sheets of paper and a felt pen.
3. Have the male students respond to the phrase, "Because I am a man,I must.." and the female students, Because I am a women, I must..."
4. Next, have them respond to the phrases, "If I were a woman, I could..."(for the boys) and "If I were a man, I could..." (for the girls).
5. Enrich the group discussions by asking questions, such as:

   Do any of the "musts" seem unfair?
   Do they have to be that way?

Is there any way to allow some of the "coulds" to happen, without necessarily being a member of the opposite sex?
What are their fears?
Which of these responses are most powerful and most widespread in our society?
What things on the list are you most glad of? Proud of?
Which would you not like to see changed?

SUGGESTED ACTIVITY 3.2.12

Comparing Females, Males and Healthy persons

Prepare three copies of the following list. Label one page "Male"; another page, "Female". and the third page " Healthy Person". Give the students a set each. Describe the list as a sort of continuum. Ask the students to indicate which set of adjectives accurately describes the word at the top of the page. They should check the appropriate space. For example, if a student feels that a male is very aggressive, he/she should check space one. If the student feels that the male is non-aggressive, he/she should check space five. If the student feels that the male is neither, check space three.

After the class has completed the three lists, tally the results and discuss. Ask the class which adjectives were the most difficult to classify. Was it easier to do the list for Male? Female? Or Healthy person? How did the description of the Healthy Person compare with that of the Male of Female?

Alternatively, the class can be divided into three small groups, with each group given the same list. One group will describe Male, another the Female, and the third a Healthy Person. The groups will need to reach a consensus in order to select the appropriate adjective score. After the groups have finished, they will return to the large group for discussion and comparison of lists.

	1	2	3	4	5	
Aggressive						Nonaggressive
Independent						Dependent
Unemotional						Emotional

Objective ____________________ Subjective

Dominant ____________________ Submissive

Not excitable ____________________ Excitable

Active ____________________ Passive

Competitive ____________________ Non-competitive

Logical ____________________ Illogical

Direct ____________________ Indirect

Feelings not easily hurt ____________________ Feelings easily hurt

Adventurous ____________________ Cautious

Never cries ____________________ Cries easily

Leader ____________________ Follower

Self-confident ____________________ Unsure

Ambitious ____________________ Not Ambitious

Handles ideas ____________________ Handles feelings

Not concerned about appearance ____________________ Concerned about appearance

Not talkative ____________________ Talkative

Blunt ____________________ Tactful

Unaware of other's feelings ____________________ Aware of other's feelings

Untidy ____________________ Neat

Loud ____________________ Quiet

Tough ____________________ Tender

SUGGESTED ACTIVITY 3.2.13

Male and Female Roles in Literature and Television

Both literature and the media can be used to facilitate

discussion on male and female roles. The images of men and women, as reflected in novels, short stories and poetry, as well as those presented on television and the theater, serve as mirrors which we can use to view ourselves and others. When presenting the class with a piece of literature or when discussing a television movie which deals in some way with the roles of men and women, ask them to consider the following questions:

How do you relate to the characters?

Do the roles of the men and women seem realistic?

Can you identify with the characters?

Do they reflect the traditional roles of men and women? How?

What are the goals of the men and women?

Do the characters fulfill your expectations in terms of what you feel a man should be? A woman should be?

Were you influenced by what you read? How does it affect your opinion about men and women?

3.3 BEING MASCULINE/FEMININE

Objective :

1. To increase the student's awareness of the stereotyped sex roles and to encourage them to notice how they compare themselves to stereotypes.

Time Required : 30 minutes

Materials : "Labels" handout, black-board or newsprint and market.

PROCEDURE

1. Explain the definitions of masculine and feminine. (Masculine= men, Feminine=women)
2. Distribute homework sheet: labels under Activity 3.2.1
3. Give the class five minutes to go over the list and assign each word in the list as either masculine or feminine.

4. Label one piece of newsprint "Masculine" and "Feminine".
5. Get the students to call out words on their lists that are feminine. Do the same with words that are masculine. list these words on the newsprint labelled accordingly.
6. As a student calls out a word,ask him/her to explain why she chose that to be masculine or feminine.
7. Ask the students for the other words that are masculine and feminine.
8. Ask the students for the basis of their choice.
9. Ask the students if they think a boy can ever be unmechanical or gentle, and if a girl can ever be strong or brave.
10. Ask the students what they think it would feel like if they had to be everything on one chart and nothing on the other.
11. Ask it any of the the girls have "masculine" traits or if any boys have "feminine" traits. Get them to talk about any problems they have because of those characteristics. (example: a tall girl; a sensitive boy)
12. Summarize the discussion by making the following points:
    - A. Stereotyped sex roles keep people from developing their natural abilities and personalities.
    - B. Sexual stereotyping is reinforced by expecting certain modes of behaviour from boys and girls, and by rejecting boys and girls who don't conform to those expectations.
    - C. To be free of sex role stereotyping, a person should recognize his/her own needs and feelings and accept that differences exist among people.

SUGGESTED ACTIVITY 3.3.1

Homework

Have students take home their completed "Labels" exercise and a copy of the homework sheet and below and request their parents to do the same exercise.

In class, the students take home compare their responses with those of their parents. This meant to validate sex stereotyping among an older generation, the parents.

HOMEWORK SHEET: "LABELS"

Instructions

Read through this list of words quickly, putting an "F" next to those that describe females and an "M" next to those that describe males.

adventurous	gossip	sexy
aggressive	good cook	soft
big		graceful
strong		
boss		hairy sweet
brave	hard	talkative
breadwinner	helpess	tall
cute		hero tender
dainty	independent	tough
domineering	innocent	unmechanical
dumb	loud	wholesome
emotional	motherly	wicked
foxy		nagging quiet
gentle	giggly	sensitive

3.4 STEREOTYPE VOTING

Objective :

1. To help students develop more understanding about masculinity and femininity.
2. To compare ideas and explore sex role stereotyping.

Time Required : 10-15 minutes

Materials : Blackboard or newsprint and pens

PROCEDURE

1. Explain to students that in order to understand how sex roles affect our lives, we need to take a look at how we define masculinity and femininity; and what some of our automatic assumptions may be that could influence self-image and relationships with others.

2. Draw the following pairs of figures on the board/newsprint and ask students to vote which figure they would label masculine and which they would label feminine (majority rules).

3. Most groups give these results:

4. If class results are the same as or similar to Step 3, tell students that most other groups of varying ages get the same results.

5. Ask students how they made their choices with each pair, pointing out what they reveal about their definitions of masculinity and femininity.

COMMENTS AND CONSIDERATIONS

There are not right or wrong answers in this activity. The teacher should be careful not to make any assumptions about how students will respond. Try not to have any expectations which can interfere with polling students about the paired figures.

MODULE 4

SEXUALLY TRANSMITTED DISEASES

4

SEXUALLY TRANSMITTED DISEASES

This is the last of a series of four modules that comprised the package entitle Adolescences Education. This module on sexually transmitted diseases discuses the various types of STD, their origin, symptoms, effects, testing and prevention and explains them in the context of social and medical problems. This particular module consists of the following lessons and their corresponding objectives:

Topics	**Objectives**
Lesson 4.1 Sexually Transmitted Diseases	(1) To increase knowledge on the various types of STD, their origin, symptoms, ef fects testing and prevention. (2) To increase understanding of STD as a medical problem. (3) To convince students that as a social and medical problem, STDs should be treated immediately.
Lesson 4.2 Information	To review and organize basic information VD about VD.
Lesson 4.3 VD Myth Game	To correct misinformation and to provide the opportunity to discuss VD

Each lesson is provided with a set of objectives and indicates the time required for teaching, the materials to be used and the set of procedure to be followed in carrying out the teaching. Information sheets to help teachers in expanding the subject, reference materials and activities/exercises for students are also provided.

4.1 SEXUALLY TRANSMITTED DISEASES (STD)

Objectives :

1. To increase knowledge on the various types of STD, their origin, symptoms, effects, tests, and prevention.
2. To increase understanding of STD as a social as well as a medical problem.
3. To convince students that as a social and medical problem STDs should be treated immediately.

Time Required : 30-45 minutes

Materials : Information Sheets

PROCEDURE

1. Lecture on the various types of STD using Information Sheet pp. (17-29). This sheet can be duplicated and distributed to the students for further study and discussion with their parents and peers. Of the various STDs, emphasize AIDS.
2. After the lecture, have the students do Activities 4.1.1, 4.1.2, 5.1.3., 4.1.4, 4.1.5, 4.1.6, 4.1.7 and 4.1.8.

INFORMATION SHEET

1. Introduction

A. Sexually transmitted diseases (STD) are diseases which usually are contracted through sexual relations.

1. STDs affect the sexual organs and can seriously affect other organs.
2. Gonorrhea and syphilis are the most common STDs. AIDS, however, is the most fatal as no cure for it has been discovered yet.

3. Sexually transmitted diseases are also known as venereal diseases.

B. STDS have reached epidemic proportions.

1. Syphilis and gonorrhea combined have the highest incidence of any reportable communicable disease. However, *the actual* numbers of cases is estimated to be three to five times the number of reported cases. In much the same way, as of 31 Jan. 1991, a total of 323,379 cases of AIDS have been reported by more than 150 countries around the world but WHO estimates that the actual number of cases may be as high as three to five times the number of reported cases.

2. Herpes II, known to be occurring at alarming rates, is not a disease which is reported to health departments, therefore, no numbers are available to document the incidence.

C. *The actual number of cases of STDs is not known.*

1. One reason for the lack of information is that some doctors are hesitant to report cases to the Health Department.

2. Many people have an STD, but have no symptoms.

3. People are often afraid, embarrassed or ashamed to seek help in a clinic.

D. *STDs are a social as well as a medical problem worldwide.*

1. There is still a lot of social stigma attached to STDs.

2. In the past it was difficult to get treatment without harassment—this attitude luckily is changing.

E. *Vaccines against STDs*

1. There is no vaccine available for syphilis or gonorrhea at this time.

2. The diseases do not cause the body to produce antibodies prevent reinfection.

3. It is possible to get STDs again and again; in the case

of herpes, the infection never leaves the body.

II. The History of STDs

A. *Historical writings indicate that STDs have been a health problem since ancient times.*

1. STDs are referred to in the Old Testament.

2. Hippocrates described syphilis-like sores in 460 B.C.

3. One theory of the origins of syphilis in Europe is that Columbus and his crew returned from the New World with syphilis; Columbus himself died from an advanced case of syphilis.

B. *STDs affected modern European history.*

1. STDs followed wherever armies travelled during wartime.

2. Charles VIII of France was the last of his dynasty as all his children were born dead from syphilis.

3. Syphilis caused other European kings to go mad, thus affecting their capabilities for governing their realms.

III. Gonorrhea

A. Gonorrhea is the most common sexually transmitted disease.

1. The bacteria which causes gonorrhea was discovered in 1870. It is called the gonococcus of Neiser named after the scientist who first discovered it.

2. Gonococci can only penetrate certain types of cells in the human body. These cells are found in the cervix, urethra, rectum, the lining of the eyelids, the throat and the vagina, including those of young girls.

3. The bacteria can live only a short time outside a warm, moist environment. However, they can live outside the body in pus for about an hour. It is feasible, but rare, to catch gonorrhea from contaminated towels, underwear and toilet seats.

4. Gonococci can live for years inside the human body.

B. *Symptoms of gonorrheal infection:*

1. 80 per cent of women and 40 per cent of men with gonorrhea are a symptomatic (they show no symptoms.)

2. For those who do exhibit symptoms, the most common is pain or burning while urinating-this is especially true of males.

3. Several days following exposure, there may be a discharge from the cervix, penis or anus, or sore throat. This discharge goes away by itself after several weeks but the disease remains, moving deeper into the reproductive system.

4. At this stage a woman may experience pain on one or both sides of her abdomen. She may have fever, nausea and vomiting and may have irregular periods.

5. In men, an abscess may develop in the prostate gland. Gonococci may then be ejaculated along with the sperm during intercourse.

C. *Long-term effects of gonorrhea.*

1. Death does not usually result from gonorrhea, but the effects may be very serious.

2. In males, untreated gonorrhea may lead to sterility due to scar tissue blocking the passage of sperm. Heart disease or gonorrheal arthritis may develop from the invasion of tissue by gonococci.

3. In females, untreated gonorrhea may lead to partial or complete blockage of the fallopian tubes by scar tissue.

   a. Partial blockage can result in ectopic pregnancy. This occurs when the sperm fertilizes the egg and instead of travelling down to the uterus to grow, the egg gets stuck and implants itself in the fallopian tube. If not diagnosed early, the tube can rupture causing a severe infection and sometimes death.

b. Complete blockage of the tubes results in sterility as the sperm cannot make their way to the egg.

4. As in males, gonorrhea in women also can cause heart disease or arthritis.

5. Pelvic Inflammatory Disease (PID) is another possible result of gonorrhea in women. This a serious condition which affects the pelvic area containing the reproductive organs. PID is treated with antibiotics. It is rarely necessary to remove the affected sexual organs to cure the disease.

   a. Intrauterine devices (IUDs) increase the possibility of developing PID.

D. *Testing and diagnosis of gonorrhea.*

1. Diagnosis of gonorrhea is determined by taking a history of sexual activity from the patient and by demonstration of gonococci from smears or cultures of urethral, cervical, throat or rectal discharge.

2. A culture involves swabbing the discharge and placing it on a special culture plate. This is incubated 16-48 hours. The culture then is examined for the presence of the gonococcus. Smears also are taken, which are stained and examined for the organism.

E. *Pregnancy and gonorrhea.*

1. Mothers inflicted with gonorrhea can pass it on to their babies during or after birth.

2. The eyes of the newborn are extremely susceptible. Infection an cause blindness. Because of this, most states require that special eye drops of silver nitrate be administered at birth.

F. *Resistance to penicillin.*

1. In general, the gonorrhea organism has become less sensitive to penicillin. Since World War II, the dos-

age of penicillin necessary to cure uncomplicated gonorrhea has increased eight-fold.

2. Recently, there have been cases in which the gonorrhea organism has been capable of producing a substance which makes penicillin ineffective against the organism. In these cases, other antibiotics must be used. The occurance of this strain of organism makes follow-up visits and test of cure particularly important.

IV. Syphilis

A. *Syphilis is less common but more dangerous than gonorrhea.*

1. Syphilis is caused by a spiral shaped organism called treponema pallidum.

2. It was discovered in 1906 by Schaudin and Hoffman. In the same year, Wassermann developed a blood test to detect syphilis.

3. Syphilis has been responsible for countless deaths and terrible suffering throughout history.

B. *There are four stages of infection with different symptoms and consequences.*

1. Primary stage:

   a. The first sign of syphilis is usually an open sore, called a chancrc, which appears three to four weeks after exposure. This sore most often occurs near the place where the spirochete entered the body.

   b. Chancres can form on the genitals, lips, fingertips, anus or mouth.

   c. Many women never know they have a chancre because it forms on the cervix or inside the vagina or rectum.

   d. Chancres are painless and disappear by themselves in one to five weeks.

e. The primary stage is very infectious. The chancre is loaded with spirochetes. These can enter the body through the pores of the skin. Transfer usually takes place during *sexual* contact, but at this stage it can occur however physical contact is made (kissing, touching, etc.)

2. Secondary stage:

   a. In this stage the organisms enter the circulatory and Iymphatic systems of the body.

   b. This occurs anywhere from zero to six months after the disappearance of the chancre.

   c. Many different kinds of symptoms are possible at this stage because the whole body is affected.

   d. Symptoms may include a rash, often visible on the palms of the hands and bottoms of the feet; chancre-like sores on the body; painful swollen joints; hair loss; and flu-like symptoms.

   e. At this stage syphilis can spread by simple physical contact such as kissing.

   f. The symptoms of this stage disappear by themselves. The disease, however, is still very active.

3. Late stage:

   a. This stage lasts three to twenty years.

   b. There are no visible symptoms.

   c. During this stage the spirochetes enter the internal organs such as the heart and brain.

   d. During this stage syphilis is no longer infectious.

4. Latest stage:

   a. This is the stage where the permanent damage to the body becomes apparent.

   b. Heart disease, crippling, blindness and insanity are possible long-term effects of syphilis.

C. *Diagnosis of Syphilis*

1. There are several blood tests for syphilis, but none are 100 per cent accurate.

2. Some tests can determine whether a person has had syphilis, but cannot indicate if the patient has been totally cured.

3. The procedure used to determine whether a patient has syphilis is as follows:

   a. A patient's history is taken to determine the possibility of exposure to syphilis.

   b. The patient is examined for visible symptoms.

   c. A laboratory examination of an extract from a lesion is done to determine presence of spirochetes.

   d. Blood tests are made for the same reasons.

   e. Other tests such as examination of spinal fluid may be necessary in latent, late or newborn cases.

D. *Syphilis and pregnancy*

1. Syphilis is transferred from mother to foetus during pregnancy.

2. Syphilis can cause deformity, blindness or death of the baby if the mother goes untreated.

3. If a woman is treated before the 16th week of pregnancy, the foetus probably won't be affected but will require close follow-up by health professionals.

V. Herpes Simplex, Type II

A. Herpes II usually occurs below the waist on or around the genitals.

1. Herpes II usually occurs below the waist on or around the genitals.

2. How Herpes is contracted is unknown at this point.

3. The true incidence of Herpes is not known as it is not reported to health departments. It is known to be increasing at an alarming rate.

4. Research indicates the Herpes may increase a women's risk of getting cervical cancer.

B. *Symptoms*

1. Multiple blister-like sores appear inside the vagina, on the external genitals, on the thighs, near the anus or on the penis.

2. These blisters rupture and become painful, open sores.

3. These open sores are believed to be very infectious.

4. The symptoms run their course and eventually disappear by themselves, but the virus remains in the skin in a "dormant" from.

5. Herpes can recur at any time. It seems most likely to come back when the body's resistance is lowered due to such things as stress, poor diets, fatigue, etc. In some people Herpes recurs on a cyclical basis as during the menstrual period.

C. *The clinician can diagnose Herpes either by the appearance of the sores or by a microscopic examination of a smear taken from a sore.*

D. *Herpes and pregnancy*

1. Herpes may cause a pregnant woman to deliver early or miscarry.

2. If a baby contracts Herpes during delivery through the birth canal, it may suffer severe illness or death. It is thought that this can occur if the mother has an active case of Herpes II at the time of delivery. Mothers with active Herpes II at the time of delivery should therefore deliver by Caesarian section to prevent the possibilities of the newborn becoming infected as it passes through the (infected) birth canal.

E. *Prevention of Herpes*

1. If condoms prevent contact with Herpes sores, they can help prevent contraction of the virus.

2. If a case is active, sex should be avoided.

3. People should stay in good physical condition eating well, getting plenty of rest and exercises.

VI. AIDS

A. *AIDS stands for Acquired Immune Deficiency Syndrome.*

1. AIDS is caused by a virus called HIV(Human Immunodeficiency Virus). HIV damages the body's immune system, leaving it unable to fight off infections and cancers.

2. The human blood consists of red blood cells and white blood cells or lymphocytes which come in B cells and T cells. Some T cells are called helper cells while the others are called suppressor cells. The helper cells help the B cells produce antibodies that fight disease-carrying organisms. On the other hand, the suppressor cells work to stop or suppressor this fight against invading germs. In people with AIDS, the suppressor cells outnumber the helper cells, leaving the immune system weak or ineffective in the fight against diseases.

3. Only five years after the syndrome was first described, 29,000 cases (as of August 1986) was reported in 71 countries around the world. The World Health Organization estimates that the actual number of cases may be as high as 400,000. In addition to cases of AIDS, five to ten million people may be infected with HIV, the virus that causes AIDS.

4. AIDS is a fatal disease that cannot yet be cured.

5. AIDS affects men, women and children as are result of, unprotected sex with an infected person, exposure to HIV infected blood, blood products, organs and tissues, transmission of the virus from mother to her

foetus or infant before, during or shortly after birth.

6. AIDS is not spread by casual contact.

B. *Symptoms of AIDS*:

1. It can take from six months to many years for a person who has been exposed to HIV to develop the disease.

2. Some people exposed to HIV may never proceed to the final stage of AIDS, but they become "carriers". Although carriers appear healthy, they can give HIV to a sexual partner or to someone they share a needle with.

3. Many of the symptoms of AIDS, are also symptoms of minor illness like colds or flu but in AIDS, these symptoms either don't go away or keep coming back.

4. These symptoms include:

   a. Unexplained weight loss greater than 10 pounds.

   b. Recurring fever and /or night sweats.

   c. Unexplained fatigue.

   d. Diarrhea.

   e. Swollen glands usually in the neck, armpits or groins.

   f. Unexplained dry cough.

   g. White spots or unusual blemished on the tongue or mouth.

   h. Pink or purple blotches or bumps on or under the skin, inside the mouth, nose, eyelids or rectum. The bumps may look like bruises but they don't go away.

C. Effect of AIDS.

1. Many people carrying the AIDS virus look and feel perfectly well for long periods of time. They may go on indefinitely this way. Some will develop a milder

form of AIDS called ARC (AIDS- related complex). ARC can include any symptoms of AIDS or it may turn into "full blown" AIDS.

2. AIDS is a fatal disease. In the U.S., about 50 per cent of patients die within 18 months of diagnosis and about 80 per cent, within 36 months. Less than 10 per cent of persons with AIDS have survived longer than three years.

3. It is not the virus itself which kills the person but the infection or cancer that develops.

4. The number one cause of death of persons with AIDS is pneumocystis carinii pneumonia (PCP), an infection of the lungs.

5. Of the cancers, Kaposi's sarcoma (KS) is the most common. It is a cancer of the tissues beneath the skin. It can also affect the lymphnodes and internal organs.

6. New evidence shows that HIV may also attack the nervous system, causing damage to the brain and spinal cord. Signs of damage may include memory loss, indifference, inability to make decisions, partial paralysis, loss of coordination and other problems in controlling the body.

D. *Testing and diagnosis of AIDS*

1. Current screening tests do not diagnose AIDS. They detect antibodies to HIV in the blood. It just shows if a person has ever been infected by the virus. It does not indicate that a person has or will get AIDS.

2. The ELISA is the easiest, cheapest and most widely used test. It is an enzyme-linked immunosorbent assay which was originally developed to screen donated blood.

3. In ELISA, a special electronic instrument measures colour changes in serum when antibodies are exposed to pieces of HIV.

4. While ELISA is very sensitive—that is , it identifies

almost all blood containing antibodies to HIV, the test is not so specific and sometimes produces false positive.

5. Research is underway to develop more accurate and less expensive tests. Results from the ELISA test can be confirmed by the more elaborate and expensive Western blood test.

E. *How AIDS are transmitted*

1. AIDS is spread by the exchange of body fluids, especially blood, organs, tissue and semen. Sexual transmission the commonest means of infection.

2. Another way of getting AIDS is by using contaminated hypodermic needles. Blood containing the virus may be left on the needle used by an AIDS person and passed on to the next user.

3. An infected woman can give AIDS to her child during pregnancy. AIDS is thought to be transmitted from mother to infant in the womb, at birth, directly after birth through close contacts or possibly while breastfeeding.

4. Homosexual and bi-sexual men, who have many sexual partners who have been infected with AIDS, are considered high-risk groups.

5. About 3 per cent of those people and hemophiliacs who have had blood transfusions have contracted AIDS.

6. Other body fluids like saliva and tears have not been shown to spread the disease.

7. Casual contact has not been shown to spread HIV. To transmit the virus, infected cells or viral particles must pass into the tissue or bloodstream of another person.

F. *Prevention of AIDS*

1. Avoid having sex with persons known or suspected to have AIDS.

2. Limit the number of sex partners.

3. Know your sex partners and ask them about their health.

4. Avoid sexual practices that can damage body tissue (i.e., anal intercourse)

5. Do not inject illegal drugs. If you do use drugs, do not share needles.

6. Do not have sex with persons who inject drugs.

7. Always use condoms when having sex, if you are unsure of the HIV status of the partner.

8. Observe public health measures such as:

   a. providing sterile needles to intravenous drug users;

   b. screening all donated blood for HIV antibodies and discarding any seropositive blood.

VII. Other sexually Transmitted Diseases

A. *Venereal warts (condylomata accuminata)*

1. These are caused y a virus.

2. They resemble regular warts but appear on the genitals.

3. Warts appear one to three months after contact.

4. Venereal warts are painless, but they spread easily by sexual contact.

5. The warts are treated with an application of a liquid chemical called podophyllin. This liquid dries the warts. It must be washed off two sex hours after application.

6. All warts must be treated simultaneously or they will spread again.

7. Condoms help prevent the spread of venereal warts.

B. *Lice and "crabs" (pediculosis)*

1. Lice are tiny insects which cling to the base of hairs on the head, body and pubic area. They feed on blood.

2. "Crab" lice are the type found in the pubic area. They may be seen upon careful inspection. The adults appear as a small insect which can frequently be seen moving, the "moving mole". The eggs are tiny and are attached to the base of the pubic hair.

3. Crabs usually cause severe itching and reproduce quickly.

4. They cannot be washed off! Special lotions or shampoos such as Kwell, A-200 and Cuprex are used for getting rid of crabs. Some of these are available, without prescription, in drugstores.

5. Crabs can be acquired from another infected person, from bedding, clothing or toilet seats.

C. *Scabies*

1. Scabies is caused by infestation with a parasite called sarcoptes scabies.

2. It is characterized by an itchy rash most usually between the fingers, on the wrists, the genitalia or the buttocks.

3. Scabies spreads through close physical contact, not necessarily sexual intercourse.

4. Itching generally starts four to six weeks after contact.

5. Scabies is treated with a cream or lotion similar to those used for crabs. These medicines require a prescription.

6. As with lice, treatment also consists of disinfection of bedding and clothing.

D. *Molluscum Contagiosum*

1. This is a viral infection of the skin, generally

involving the genital area, the thighs, lower abdomen and other areas.

2. It appears as a small, white swelling, with a "dimple" in the middle which occurs in groups.

3. There are few, if any, symptoms.

4. Treatment consists of extruding the center or with administration of phenol. Treatment should be performed by a health professional.

E. *Vaginitis*

1. Vaginitis is a condition that causes local irritation of the vaginal wall and cervix caused by one of several different organisms. Only some of these organisms are known to be sexually transmitted.

2. Symptoms generally include vaginal discharge and irritation (itch, pain, discomfort).

3. Diagnosis is made by a smear of the vaginal (or cervical) discharge or by culture.

4. The most common organisms which cause vaginitis are candida albican (a yeast), trichomonas (a parasite) and corynebacterium vaginale (a bacteria). These infections generally respond well to adequate therapy.

5. Of the above organisms, only trichomonas infections require concurrent therapy of both sexual partners. Sometimes the male is treated for corynebacterium infection as well.

F. *Nonspecific (nongonococcal) urethtritis (NSU or NGU)*

1. This is a condition of males characterized by penile discharge and sometimes by burning on urination or an itching sensation.

2. Diagnosis is generally one of exclusion: the smear and culture for gonorrhea are both negative.

3. Causes include infection with chlamydia trachomitis (an organism between a virus and a bacteria), myco-

plasma (a bacteria) and others.

4. NSU or NGU which follows adequate treatment for gonorrhea is termed postgonococcal urethritis (PGU). The cause for this is unknown, but is thought to be an infection acquired at the same time as gonorrhea, but having a longer incubation period (period between infection and onset of symptoms).

5. Nongonococcal urethritis also may be acquired from a sexual partner.

6. The above infections can generally be treated with adequate doses of an appropriate antibiotic.

G. *The "tropical" STDs*

1. This group includes lymphogranulmoa venereum, ganuloma inquinale and chancroid.

2. These diseases occur most frequently in the tropics and subtropics.

H. *New additions to the STD list*

1. As sexual practices change, so do the disease which are transmitted through sexual intercourse.

2. The practice of oral sex is increasing, and so are the rates of some of the diseases which enter the body through the mouth. These diseases are liver and intestinal infection formerly thought to spread through food infected by chronic carriers or through needles.

3. These diseases include typhoid fever, shigella and ameobic dysentery and hepatitis (both "infectious" and "serum").

4. The intestinal infections are most easily transmitted through oral anal or oral-genital contact.

5. Treatment for some of these diseases is lacking. Some of these diseases have a "carrier state" with no outward appearance of disease, thus, there is no way to tell if a person has STD.

VIII. Prevention

A. *Restrict sexual activities*: The epidemic spread of sexually transmitted diseases is due in large part to increasing numbers of persons having multiple sexual partners.

B. *The use of mechanical barriers*: Condoms prevent skin-to-skin contact and are thus helpful in preventing the transmission of some of the diseases.

C. *Local agents*

1. Some of the contraceptive and vaginal creams, foams and jellies help reduce the chance of acquiring a STD. None are "proven" effective, and there is no reliable information on dosage and timing of application.

2. Washing with soap and water before and after sex is an important deterrent to the spread of STD.

3. Urinating after sex cleans the urethra.

D. *Prophylactic antibiotics*: This route has been disappointing- there is no "morning after pill".

E. *Vaccination*: Again, there is no vaccination against the STDs. In only a very few cases (e.g., typhoid) does having a STD give natural immunity, thus one can catch them again and again.

F. *Change in attitude*

1. This, coupled with health education, is one of the current main thrusts. The embarrassment, shame and guilt often associated with the STDs lead to delays in treatment, neglect of informing partners and spread of disease.

2. If people are knowledgeable of signs and symptoms of STDs, seek out early diagnosis and treatment, inform their partners of the necessity for treatment, and refrain from sex until they know they are no longer infectious. It will stop the spread of STDs.

SUGGESTED ACTIVITY 4.1.1

Read the following and fill in as many blanks as you can:

1. Two common sexual transmitted diseases (STD), also known as Venereal Diseases (VD) are:........................and................
2. The virus that causes AIDS is ....

   The germ that causes syphilis is.........................

   The germ that causes gonorrhoea is..............................
3. People contract STD Through..............................
4. Which of the following statements is correct? Encircle the letter of the correct answers.

   4.1 (a) The germs causing STD spread only by direct skin to skin, skin to mucosa contact between people.

   (b) The germs causing STD can spread through dirty toilet seats, door handles and dirty bedsheets.

   (c) The germs causing STD can spread through dirty clothes, dirty plates and glasses.

   4.2 Early signs of gonorrhea in men.

   _______ (a) fever and joint pains.

   _______ b) discharge of pus from the penis.

   _______ (c) burning pain when passing urine.

   _______ (d) sores on the penis.

   4.3 Early signs of gonorrhea in women are:

   _______ (a) Pus of discharge from the vagina a few days after sexual intercourse.

   _______ (b) brown discharge.

   _______ (c) bleeding off and on.

4.4 Signs of AIDS are;

_______ (a) diarrhea

_______ (b) pus from the vagina and penis

_______ (c) fever

_______ (d) bleeding

4.5 Early signs of syphilis are:

_______ (a) painless ulcer on the private parts

_______ (b) pus from the penis

_______ (c) discharge from the penis

_______ (d) rash on the private parts

_______ (e) rash all over the body.

4.6 If untreated, gonorrhea can lead to:

_______ (a) fever and painful inflammation of the internal sex organs.

_______ (b) brain damage

_______ (c) painful blockage of flow of urine in men.

_______ (d) sterility (i.e. unable to have babies).

4.7 If untreated, syphilis can lead to:

_______ (a) damage to the heart and heart and failure.

_______ (b) damage to joints and arthritis.

_______ (c) damage to the brain and insanity.

_______ (d) infection of babies of women suffering from the disease.

4.8 AIDS it is transmitted by:

_______ (a) casual contact.

_______ (b) body fluids like saliva and tears.

_______ (c) sexual intercourse.

_______ (d) heredity.

5. Write down three important ways of preventing people from getting STD.

a)

b)

c)

SUGGESTED ACTIVITY 4.1.2

Discussion questions

1. Why don't people always tell their contacts that they might have STDs?
2. If we've been able to wipe out other communicable diseases, why haven't we been able to wipe out STDs?
3. How can you use the mass media to campaign against STD?
4. What effect would it have on our society if STDs were wiped out?
5. What is the classic stereotype of someone that has had STDs? Is it accurate?
6. How do you ask someone if he has STD?

SUGGESTED ACTIVITY 4.1.3

Incomplete sentences

Direction: Complete the following:

1. STDs are........
2. People who get STDs are.......
3. If I found out I have an STD, I will.....

SUGGESTED ACTIVITY 4.1.4

Continuums/Values voting

What do you think about the following:

1. People should be required to have a test for STDs every year.
2. All men and women should be tested for syphilis before they get married.
3. Parents should be told if their teenage son or daughter has STD.

SUGGESTED ACTIVITY 4.1.5

Advice column

Dear....................,

I have a pretty serious problem and I don't know who else to turn to for help. You see, I was having some terrible pains in my stomach and I went to the emergency room because I thought I might have had appendicitis. the doctor asked me a lot of questions, examined me, and told me that I probably have gonorrhea. He did a test and told me to call back for the results.

The problem is, if I do have it, what will I tell my boyfriend? He will get it from me, won't he? I feel so terrible, I know it must be all my fault.

Worried and Waiting

P.S. I swear he's the ***only*** *one!*

SUGGESTED ACTIVITY 4.1.6

Small Group Review

This exercise is good for following up a film or lecture. It allows students to work together to review and reinforce their newly acquired information.

Materials:

Newsprint, felt pens

Assorted pamphlets on STDs (can usually be obtained from the local health department).

Time: 30-40 minutes

Procedure:

1. Divide the class into groups of four to six students. Give each group a newsprint.
2. Distribute pamphlets on various STDs to all the groups.
3. Assign all groups one or two of the following topics:

Symptoms	Complications
Testing	Incubation period
Treatment	Effects on pregnancy

4. Tell each group to divide its newsprint into columns, one each for gonorrhea, syphilis, herpes, and AIDS. Tell the groups that they will have about ten minutes to go through the pamphlets and write down the facts about their topics as they pertain to syphilis, gonorrhea, herpes, and AIDS.
5. At the end of the ten minutes, ask the groups to give their reports to the class.

SUGGESTED ACTIVITY 4.1.7

Match the STD in Column A with their corresponding definitions in Column B.

Column A STD	*Column B* DEFINITIONS
1. AIDS 2. Gonorrhea 3. Syphilis 4. Herpes II	A. This is a condition of males characterized by penile discharge and sometimes a burning sensation during urination and itchiness.
	B. A viral infection of the skin which appears as small, white swollen growths with a dimple in the middle, and occurs in groups in the genital area, the thighs, lower abdomen and other areas.
5. Venereal warts	C. Regular warts which appear on the genitals and are caused by virus.

6. Scabies	D. It is caused by a virus called Human Immunodeficiency Virus (HIV) which damages the body's immune system destroying its ability to fight off infections and cancer.
7. Vaginitis	E. It is caused by a gonococci which penetrates the cells found in the cervix, urethra, rectum, the lining of the eyelids, the throat and the vagina.
8. Molluscum Contagiosum	F. A spiral shaped organism called Treponema pallidum causes painless chancre sore on or in the genitals, anus, mouth or throat.
9. Lice and "Crabs"	G. It is a local irritation of the vaginal wall and cervix caused by one of several, different organisms.
10. Nonspecific Urethritis	H. A viral infection related to Herpes I which causes the common cold sore.
	I. Characterized by an itchy rash usually between the fingers, on the wrists, the genitalia, or buttocks
	j. Tiny insects which cling to the base of hairs on the head, body and pubic area.

SUGGESTED ACTIVITY 4.1.8

Role Play: City Council Meeting

This is a special role play designed to help the class become aware of some of the ways by which a community can work towards eradicating STDs. At the same time, students are guided in studying some of the difficulties involved in formulating a programme.

1. Select seven volunteers to play the roll of members of the City Council.
2. Tell them they are faced with a problem. The City Council of your town needs to control an epidemic of STDs among the teenage population. According to the national health department, one out of five graduating seniors has already contracted STD. The City Council is holding a special meeting in order to find ways of controlling the epidemic.
3. Every Council member will be given a slip of paper indicating his/her number as a member and attitude towards the problem.

Council Member #1: You believe that if the teenagers can be convinced to abstain from sex, much of the problem will go away.

Council Member #2: You still need to be convinced that the situation is a big problem.

Council Member #3: You think that it is mainly the poor and unhygienic people who contract STDs.

Council Member #4: You are concerned about this problem, having once had gonorrhea yourself.

Council Member #5: You would like to see STDs eradicated. You realize the seriousness of the problem and you want to see the Council come up with solutions.

Council Member #6: You are determined to get re-elected and you hesitate to take a strong stand on sex education, although you feel that it is the key issue, because of the bad publicity it might generate.

Mayor: It interests you to have different ideas brought into the open and discussed. You have thought about the value of education, media, free clinics, condoms in vending machines, special STD weeks, etc., but you feel that the "STD attack plan" has to come from the group as a whole. You would like to see them come to a group decision today.

4. When assigning students their respective roles, make it clear that while their attitudes are already defined on the special role slips, they are encouraged to expand on these as they wish.

5. Have the Mayor open the meeting by stating his growing concern over the rising STD rates. Have him/her ask the Council members for any comments or ideas.

6. The rest of the class should act as "concerned members of the community". Tell them that they may ask the Council members questions and offer suggestions, if called upon by the Mayor.

(You can also assign some of the audience other roles such

as country health officer, a high school teacher, a religious leader, a concerned parent, teenagers, and so on).

7. Allow the role play as much time as can be sustained by the energy and interest of the class.

8. Discuss the experience.

4.2 VD INFORMATION REVIEW

Objective : To review and organize basic information about VD

Time Required :20 minutes

Materials : Blackboard or newsprint with markers

PROCEDURE

1. Point out that information on VD can sometimes be confusing. Thus this activity will concentrate on basic, important information about VD.

2. List the following items on the board/newsprint, leaving enough space for the answers.

A. 4 main types of VD:	Gonorrhea	Syphilis	Herpes II	AIDS
B. Transmission:				
C. Symptoms:				
D. Effects:				
E. Treatment:				
F. Prevention:				

3. Starting with the first item, ask the students for any information they have on the various aspects of VD. Write down their answers.

4. The completed grid should include the following:

   A. 4 main types: Gonorrhea, Syphilis, Herpes II, AIDS

   B. Transmission: Sexual intercourse (95 per cent); other physical contact (5 per cent).

C. Symptoms: Sores on or near sexual organs, unusual discharge, pain or burning sensation during urination. Abdominal pain, rash, loss of hair, symptoms may not be noticeable.

D. Effects : Sterility, miscarriage, stillbirth, birth defects, blindness, insanity, death.

E. Treatment: Antibiotics (no treatment for Herpes II, a virus), local community resources (country health department).

F. Prevention: Abstinence, exclusive sexual partners, use of condom.

5. Spend a few minutes discussing other STDs, such as crabs, scabies, and vaginitis.

SUGGESTED ACTIVITY 4.2.1

This activity may be difficult for the teacher who is accustomed to a more detailed presentation about VD. The information-sharing grid is designed to review basic information when time is limited and the teacher wants to carry out activities which address the affective as well as cognitive domains. It is important to keep in mind that giving too much information may be more confusing than elightening for young people. Three main points to emphasize are: symptoms, treatment (including local services), and prevention. However, if the teacher wants to go into more detailed discussions about the other STD, Information Sheet on pp. 17-29 should be used to test the knowledge of the students after the discussion.

Sexually Transmitted Diseases

Type	Gonorrhea	Syphilis	Herpes	II Aids	Trichomonas	Monillia	Vaginitis	Crabs/ Scabies	Nsu/ Ngu
Transmission									
Symptoms									
Effects									
Treatment									
Prevention									

4.3 VD MYTH GAME

Objectives : To correct misinformation on and to provide the opportunity to discuss VD.

Time Required : 35 minutes

Materials : Myth/truth statements on 3X5 index cards, answer key.

PROCEDURE

1. Prior to the class, write each statement number regarding myths or truths about VD on an index card.

2. In introducing the exercise, explain that belief in a number of myths about VD has contributed to the continuing epidemic. To clear up these myths and to allow the student an opportunity to communicate about VD, the students will play a myth game.

3. Divide the students into small groups (4-6 students each).

4. Divide the cards containing myth and truth statements about VD evenly among the small groups.

5. Have the students take turns reading the cards out loud. After a statement is read, the group discusses it and decides whether it is a truth or myth. This process continues until all the cards are covered. Approximately one minute per card is allowed. One group member is appointed as recorder and he/she uses a sheet with numbers 1-18. The team's answers (T=truth; M=myth) are written down and are drawn to indicate the statements for which more information is required.

6. When all the groups have finished Round 1, they are requested to pass their cards in a clockwise motion to the next group. Do this carefully so that the cards do not get mixed up.

7. The process is resumed. There are as many rounds as there are groups.

8. The teacher reads the number of a statement and says whether it is a truth or myth. Students correct their an-

swer sheets as the teacher goes down the list. They are told that anytime their group misses an answer they should raise their hands.

9. In case of an incorrect answer from any group, the statement is read in full and the answer is more thoroughly discussed.

10. The procedure of reading the numbers and the answers is repeated until all 18 questions are covered.

11. If time allows, ask the groups to call out the number of questions which they had started. Additional information can be provided at this time.

SUGGESTED ACTIVITY 4.3.1

Circulate among small groups to be sure that all students are participating as much as possible. It is important to encourage students to participate so they can get some experience in discussion about VD.

1. **Birth control pills do not prevent VD.** **Myth**

   Actually, the pill makes women who are exposed to gonorrhea more susceptible to infection, because the pill changes the PH balance of the vagina from acidic to basic, which is a more hospitable environment for gonorrhea germs.

2. **People can get VD from doorknobs, toilet seats, drinking foundations, swimming pools.** **Myth**

   VD germs do not live for long outside of the human body-they are very sensitive to temperature and light. However, other STDs (sexually transmitted diseases) like crabs, and scabies, could be gotten from toilet seats, towels, clothes, bedding.

3. **If the symptoms go away, you don't need to see a doctor.** **Myth**

   Even if the symptoms go away, the person almost always is still infected and may very likely be contagious as well.

4. **Once you've had VD you're immune to it, and you won't ever have to worry about it again.** **Myth**

There is no immunity to any of these diseases. It's possible to get them over again. Repeated infections increase the possibility of scars tissue in the fallopian tubes or vas deferens which can cause sterility or sub-fertility.

5. **Homosexuals don't get VD.** Myth

   Anybody who is sexually active can get VD. VD germs can be passed through sexual contact between persons of the same sex, as well as between persons of the opposite sex.

6. **VD can be considered a social, as well as medical problem.** Truth

   Many people are ashamed or embarrassed when they find out they have VD. Sometimes they do not tell their partner/partners. This lack of communication has contributed greatly to the spread of VD.

7. **The majority of people who get VD are over 30.** Myth

   75 per cent of all reported cases involved people between the ages of 15 and 30.

8. **Clean people are less likely to get VD.** Myth

   VD germs cannot be washed away. Anyone who is exposed can get VD.

9. **Pregnant women can infect their babies with VD.** Truth

   Syphilis can be passed through the placenta to the foetus causing birth defects, miscarriages and stillbirths. Gonorrhea and Herpes simplex Type II can be passed to the baby at birth and can also cause serious birth defects and sometimes death.

10. **Men and women always have symptoms if they have gonorrhea.** Myth

    An estimated 40 per cent of males and 80 per cent of females infected with gonorrhea have no recognizable symptoms.

11. **If you go for VD treatment, you are asked to name your contact/contacts.** Truth

    This is done so that they can be tested or treated themselves. The name of the person who listed them as contacts is never mentioned. It is totally confidential.

12. **A serious concern about VD is that some strains are becoming increasingly resistant to penicillin.** Truth

There is one form of gonorrhea which is totally resistant to penicillin, but it can still be cured by another antibiotic, spectinomycin. However, other strains are becoming increasingly resistant. Herpes Simplex II, a virus, is incurable. People who are allergic to penicillin are also treated with antibiotics.

13. **Syphilis can cause insanity and blindness** Truth

In the later stages, untreated syphilis can attack the brain and other vital organs leading to insanity, blindness, paralysis, paralysis, death.

14. **Women who are infected with Herpes Simplex II are more likely to get cervical cancer later in life.** Truth

For this reason, women with Herpes Simplex II should be careful to have a Pap smear test done every six to 12 months, according to their doctor's instructions.

15. **A person with VD symptoms may have another kind of infection which is not VD** Truth

Painful urination in both males and females may be a symptom of a urinary tract or bladder infection which may or may not be related to a VD infection. Vaginal pain, itching, burning, and/or discharges may be symptoms of a vaginal infection which may or may not be related to a VD infection. The only way to know for sure is to see a physician.

16. **Condoms provide 100 per cent protection from VD.** Myth

It has been estimated that condoms could prevent 95 per cent of all VD cases. Condoms only protect when all infected areas of the body are prevented from coming in contact with the partner's body.

17. If two people don't have VD to begin with, and they only have intercourse with each other, they'll never get VD. Truth

Only when one or both partners has sexual relations with other people who have VD can the original couple be exposed to VD.

18. Abstinence ensures 100 per cent protection from VD. Myth

95 per cent of all cases of VD are gotten through sexual intercourse. However, approximately 5 per cent of all cases can be gotten through other forms of close contact (kissing, touching a sore). A person who is practicing abstinence might still become infected in this way, although the chances are very slim.